THE MIND AND WORK
OF PAUL KLEE

FULL MOON, 1919

Stangl Gallery, Munich

THE MIND AND WORK OF
PAUL KLEE

by

WERNER HAFTMANN

PRAEGER — NEW YORK

BOOKS THAT MATTER

Published in the United States of America
in 1954 by Frederick A Praeger, Inc.,
Publishers, 105 West 40th Street,
New York 18, N.Y.

Library of Congress Catalog Card Number: 54–11543

Printed in Great Britain

CONTENTS

INTRODUCTION *page* 13

I. EARLY YEARS 19

II. YEARS OF APPRENTICESHIP 34

III. THE EUROPEAN PHALANX 51

IV. THE GIFT OF COLOUR 63

V. THE MASTER AT THE BAUHAUS 76

VI. THE PEDAGOGICAL SKETCHBOOK 92

VII. WAYS OF STUDYING NATURE 110

VIII. A PICTURE IS BORN 125

IX. THE HEART OF A PICTURE 146

X. THE HANDLING OF FORM 165

XI. TOWARDS THE ANGELS 191

BIBLIOGRAPHY 207

INDEX 209

ILLUSTRATIONS

COLOUR PLATES

FULL MOON, 1919 *frontispiece*

HIGH WAY AND BYWAYS, 1929 *facing page* 146

GROWTH OF NOCTURNAL PLANTS, 1922 170

MONOCHROME PLATES

1. WATERCOLOUR PAINTED ON GLASS, 1907 38
Collection F. Laurens, Cincinnati

2. THE NIESEN, 1915 39
Private Collection, Bern (Rupf) (*Photograph Felbermeyer, Rome*)

3. DEMON OVER THE BOATS, 1916 42
Museum of Modern Art, New York (*Photograph Soichi Sunami*)

4. MILDLY TROPICAL LANDSCAPE, 1918 43
Private Collection, Stuttgart

5. DANCE OF THE VEILS, 1920 64
Collection Ibach, Munich (*Photograph Czako, Munich*)

6. AUTUMNAL PLACE, 1921 65
Private Collection, Munich (*Photograph Grete Eckert, Munich*)

7. FISHES, 1921 80
Private Collection, Hamburg (*Photograph E. M. Czako, Gauting*)

8. EXERCITIUM IN BLUE AND ORANGE, 1924 81
Private Collection, Munich (*Photograph Grete Eckert, Munich*)

9. THE MOUNT OF THE BULL, 1923 116
Private Collection (*Photograph E. M. Czako, Gauting*)

ILLUSTRATIONS

10. MOCKING-BIRD'S SONG, 1924   *facing page* 117
Klee Foundation (*Photograph Czako, Munich*)

11. BIRD-GARDEN, 1924   124
Collection Ibach, Munich (*Photograph Czako, Munich*)

12. MOUNTAIN CARNIVAL, 1924   125
Klee Foundation (*Photograph Czako, Munich*)

13. MOONRISE, 1925   128
Private Collection, Munich (*Photograph Grete Eckert, Munich*)

14. INSCRIPTION, 1926   129
Guggenheim Foundation, New York

15. ALL ROUND THE FISH, 1926   144
Museum of Modern Art, New York (*Photograph Soichi Sunami*)

16. OCEANIC LANDSCAPE, 1929   145
Private Collection, Munich (*Photograph Grete Eckert, Munich*)

17. FOOL IN A TRANCE, 1929   150
Private Collection, Wiesbaden (*Photograph E. M. Czako, Gauting*)

18. HOVERING, 1930   151
Klee Gesellschaft, Bern

19. THE SEALED LADY, 1930   154
Collection Vowinckel, Munich (*Photograph Grete Eckert, Munich*)

20. HOW IT ALL GROWS! 1932   155
Klee Foundation

21. REVOLT OF THE VIADUCT, 1937   160
Kunsthalle, Hamburg (*Photograph C. A. Holbach, Ratingen*)

22. NORTH ROOM, 1932   161
Klee Gesellschaft, Bern (*Photograph Hinz, Basle*)

23. FIGURE IN A GARDEN, 1937   176
Klee Foundation (*Photograph Czako, Munich*)

24. GREYBEARD AND THE COASTLINE, 1938   177
Klee Foundation (*Photograph Czako, Munich*)

25. LAND WITCHES, 1938   180
Klee Foundation (*Photograph Czako, Munich*)

26. FLOWER, 1938   181
Collection Hilla Rebay

ILLUSTRATIONS

27. PARK NEAR LU, 1938   *facing page* 188
Klee Foundation

28. WEEPING WOMAN, 1939   189
Klee Foundation (*Photograph Czako, Munich*)

29. DARK VOYAGE, 1940   196
Klee Gesellschaft, Bern (*Photograph E. M. Czako, Gauting*)

30. TWILIGHT BLOOMS, 1940   197
Klee Foundation (*Photograph Czako, Munich*)

31. DRUMMER, 1940   204
Klee Foundation (*Photograph Czako, Munich*)

32. DEATH AND FIRE, 1940   205
Klee Foundation (*Photograph Czako, Munich*)

LINE BLOCKS IN THE TEXT

ILLUSTRATION FOR VOLTAIRE'S 'CANDIDE', 1911   *page* 13

BERN, 1910   20

CONCERT ON A BRANCH, 1921   24

THE BEETLE, 1925   31

AN ALARMING MOMENT, 1912   44

ILLUSTRATION FOR VOLTAIRE'S 'CANDIDE', 1911   48

KAIRUAN (SKETCH), 1914   67

GOING TO THE DANCE OF THE FLY-BY-NIGHTS, 1922   75

HIGHER, THEN DWINDLING (ILLUSTRATION FOR
    C. CORRINTH'S 'POTSDAMER PLATZ'), 1919   79

THE STAG, 1918   80

DRAWING WITH THE PAUSE-SIGN, 1918   91

PLAYFUL WATER, 1935   114

ILLUSTRATIONS

FISH IN THE BROOK, 1926   *page* 117

PLANTS, FOR EARTH AND AIR, 1920   123

INCLINED BLOOMS, 1927   136

FLYING SEED, 1925   152

THE BIG DOME, 1927   156

CAT ACROBATS, 1912   169

CITY OF THE LAGOONS, 1927   184

OVER AND UP, 1931   193

INSIDE THE BODY'S CAVERN, 1940   195

Illustration for Voltaire's 'Candide', 1911

INTRODUCTION

I had better begin with a confession: I did not know Klee,
I never met him; I have only encountered his pictures.
However, ten years after his death, it suddenly seemed to
me important to talk about these encounters, both by way
of a tribute and out of gratitude to the painter whose work
has taught me during the last twenty and more years, how
much art can do to inspire future generations to take advantage courageously of a wider field of artistic activity.

This book then deals with a series of encounters. It is not an

13

attempt to enter into a controversial discussion of the pros and
cons of modern art. For any such discussion depends on having
first thoroughly understood the impulses and achievements of
those individual masters who have made modern art. To-day
an excess of philosophical concepts obscures our vision, so that
pictures and the people who paint them are no longer clearly
seen. We must therefore try to turn our attention to the expressive powers of the pictures themselves. For only by listening to their silent communications can we hope to reach the
spiritual source whence they and their messages emanate. That
source is a moment of becoming, a stage at which a personality
grows active and creative, by bringing into action a particular
kind of intelligence which I should like to call 'pictorial thinking'. This 'pictorial thinking' is also a process of appropriating
ordering, realizing and expressing a man's spiritual attitude
to the entire world. It is expressed in a special kind of language, in the case of painting a language of colour and form, and
has an exact logic of its own. The ways of this 'pictorial thinking' lead far beyond the bounds of a man's spiritual biography
especially if he was born a painter and used his work to experience and, in so far as grace was given to him, come to terms
with life. The spectator therefore must first approach pictures
of this type along the same paths as the artist, for only in this
way can he experience the inner compulsion that determined
the growth of each work of art. The artist's philosophy may
then be revealed at the outcome of his quest, but it cannot be a
starting point. I have attempted to describe the paths Paul
Klee followed in his pictorial thinking.

Now I am a whole generation younger than Paul Klee.
That is to say, I was not exposed to the warmth and vitality
of his living personality. I have known only the potent illumination of his work, which already means that I see the

life of the man himself against something of a gilt background
of legend. As a result his achievement and influence may appear graver and more remote perhaps than those of his
friends who were exposed to the magic and lovableness of his
personality will wish to remember. But I think that Will
Grohmann's long-awaited book on Paul Klee (the publication
of which I anticipate with the greatest pleasure) will tell us a
great deal about the magic, the gaiety and the goodness that
irradiate Klee's art. If I have been fortunate, some of his
radiance may have found its way into the pages of my little
book, though this has not been my primary concern. My aim
has been rather to examine Paul Klee's thought and personality with such detachment that the extreme sincerity of
his pictorial aims would become apparent. I have sought to
concentrate on his strict respect for form, and on his hard but
successful struggle to find a means of communicating the
world through which man expresses himself, because Klee
believed that man was endowed with a creative urge in order
to create new realities, 'Realities with art, which make life
larger than it usually appears'.

Paul Klee succeeded in making us aware that the visible
world in the form we know is not the only world that exists.
Not far away from it, comparable to it, but on a parallel plane
of its own, there exists a world through which man expresses
himself. That is where his thoughts have their roots. But art is
the expression, in a generalized form, of intense desires which
each in turn goad mankind to action. The artistic activity of
our century has been inspired by an intense curiosity about
the world of self-expression. And Klee's fame is based on the
fact that he has revealed this in the sphere of pictorial art. Let
us then try, by reasoning, to analyse his pictorial achievement,
and then perhaps we may succeed in laying bare the terrain

in which his own activity had its roots, thus allowing him to enrich our own lives with a new capacity for development. Klee lit a torch which must be handed on to others. This book, therefore, is not a picture-book, but a book to be read. In so far as it records the hard struggle and the principles which underlie Klee's art, it will destroy the legend that this art is a unique accident of personality, that there can be no sequel to it, and that it is not valid as an example. This judgment, which one hears only too often, is tantamount to condemning Klee to death. In reality, however, Klee's place to-day is in the very midst of the most vital younger European painters. He is, in fact, the real moral criterion for the painting of our day. His spirit and his ideas should by rights inspire all present-day art schools and academies.

Klee's life and achievement are indeed closely interwoven. Like a plant, he was subject to the laws of vital growth. The various stages of his life are as marked as the rings in the life of a tree; so we are continually forced back to biographical facts. But in order not to let biography get the upper hand, I have always endeavoured first of all to listen to what his pictures have to say about life. Subsequently however I have had the great satisfaction of finding how their messages correspond with passages in Klee's theoretical writings, letters, and diaries as well as with known biographical data.

This little book has been written calmly, and in no combative spirit. There are many people whose assistance I have to acknowledge, above all that of the collectors of Klee's works who have so readily shown me their treasures, especially Frau Edith Vowinckel-Diel. Also the members of the former Klee Gesellschaft in Bern, especially Dr. Meyer Benteli, who made it possible for me to examine papers and pictures belonging to the Klee Stiftung, and arranged for me to visit private collections in Bern. Many of Klee's pupils too have talked to me about their master, in particular Felix Klee and Fritz Winter, who looked through his Dessau lecture notes with me. Dr. Lehmann-Brockhaus, librarian of the Central Institute for the History of Art in Munich, spared no pains to procure for me such books as I needed, many of them difficult to obtain. I dedicate this book to the Director of the Hamburg Kunsthalle, Professor Dr. Carl Georg Heise, on his sixtieth birthday, as a modest tribute from a younger man who has gained immeasurably by his kindness and unfailing assistance.

Chapter I

EARLY YEARS

A house full of cats and music—such was the home of the
painter Paul Klee. It was in Münchenbuchsee, near
Bern. A suburban house with a little garden, full of
lovingly tended flowers, and a shady terrace where
many a visitor would linger. The household was subject to the
tyranny of its spoilt feline inhabitants. This gave to the whole
milieu a quaintly Bohemian air, yet it was merely a cosy background to a severe spiritual life and a strict artistic discipline.
The house owed its distinctive atmosphere to Klee's father.
Hans Klee was born in 1849 in Thüringen, and at an early
age was offered a post at the Teachers' College in Bern to
teach music and singing. There he remained for more than
fifty years. A musician and a teacher by profession, but a
musicologist by disposition, Paul Klee's father was distinguished by a keen, uncompromising critical sense which was
only slightly mellowed by a sarcastic, even scurrilous, sense of
humour.

On 18th December 1879, Paul Klee was born in Münchenbuchsee. His mother, Ida Maria Klee-Frick, was then twenty-
four years old. On her mother's side, her family came from the
south of France, although an unexplained family tradition referred to more remote origins in North Africa. This is not

19

without significance, for the whole of Paul Klee's art is pervaded by a peculiar Oriental-Mediterranean strain. This was also true of Klee himself; with his great, brown Bedouin eyes, and dark hair, he seemed half-oriental, half-Arab, or something of the sort. His mother, too, was very musical, and had been trained as a music teacher. It was she who encouraged her son from an early age to take up music, herself accompanying the often reluctant child to his first violin lessons.

Bern, 1910

Thus Klee could claim to have been born partially Swiss, but he never acquired Swiss nationality, for his father, in his sarcastic, humorous way, never thought of paying the sum required to give him Swiss nationality. Berne meant much to Klee, however; he spent his whole youth there and always spoke a robust Bernese German, which sometimes contrasted strangely with his mysterious, almost magical appearance. Klee's art, however, developed independently of modern Swiss painting, for it followed the main trends of German and French art. It was European from the very outset.

Klee's limitless fantasy, which also embraced the world of the Orient, was nourished at a very early age. From his earliest childhood he heard colourful Oriental fairy-tales told to him by his maternal grandmother; and as she illustrated many of them herself, she soon awakened in him an inclination to draw and paint. Such were the origins of his first fantastic illustrative drawings, which were closely related to the fairy-tale world about which he had heard as a child. Nothing was drawn from nature. Then, in a restaurant owned by an uncle, there were little tables with beautiful marble tops whose fine veinings encouraged his fantasy to further flights. He would stare at them for hours on end, until the elaborate veining of the marble induced dream-images no less elaborate. This was all of the greatest significance for Klee, who would often talk about it in later years, and remark that, when his grandmother died, before he was six, 'he was left behind, an orphaned artist'.

Then his musical education began. He studied the violin and soon made such remarkable progress that, when he was barely ten, he played in concerts at Bern as an extra member of the orchestra. It was then that he acquired his astonishing mastery of the technique and expressive power of his instrument, and also his extensive knowledge of the literature of music. Until 1906, when he left Bern, Paul Klee played more or less regularly at concerts given by the municipal orchestra. And later, in Munich, Weimar and Dessau, concerts of chamber music at the Klee home were among the greatest musical pleasures of his friends, who did not need to be invited since Klee had a passion for music. He knew everything, attended every concert, and followed the development of modern music with burning interest. His diaries contain more about concerts and his other musical experiences than about anything else. Bach, and particularly Mozart, were in his opinion the greatest composers, and there are musicians who claim that they have never heard Mozart played in a bolder or more congenial way than by Paul Klee. And it was because Klee was such an excellent musician, that he saw so clearly the profound distinction between music and painting. Admittedly he would have agreed, in a general sense, with Gauguin's statement that 'the new art based on colour is entering a musical phase', or with Van Gogh's suggestion that painting seemed to be getting nearer 'to music than to sculpture'. But the comparison between musical harmony and the harmony of coloured forms which has become increasingly important ever since the days of Gauguin, from Matisse to Delaunay, from the Jugendstil to Hoelzel and Kandinsky, had no more than a vague, aphoristic value for Klee. Only in terms of rhythm could he visualize any strict comparison. In this connection it is worth noting that Klee was once observed by one of his pupils in Dessau marching absent-mindedly, but as though under a spell, in time to the music of a passing band right down the middle of the slabs of a concrete pavement. As soon as his pupil spoke to him he broke off, alarmed and embarrassed, and in the course of the ensuing conversation about the suggestive power of the passing music and the rhythm of the slabs of concrete, Klee immediately set himself and his pupil the problem of expressing this rhythmic relationship in pictorial terms. The next day, Klee produced his solution: a rush of flowing lines set off against a hard rhythm of rectangular forms on the left hand side. This sort of musical, rhythmical experience was certainly at the root of many of Klee's pictures, right up to that wonderful late picture, 'Heroic Bowing'[1] of 1938. But the purity of Klee's thought prevented any obliteration of frontiers. Anything that he experienced, even in the musical field, had first of all to insist on making itself felt (even after a thorough purging) on the plane of the pictorial means, before it assumed form as a picture.

Besides all this music-making and drawing Klee of necessity had to submit to the unpleasant experience of being educated,[2] a process which, as he himself said, 'became every year more disagreeable'. It was the end of the century, when new ideas about education and a growing appeal to youth made for a particularly tense atmosphere between the conservative body of teachers and their pupils. In his cautious, gaily ironical way, Klee was naturally on the side of the attackers. He only made an exception for his Greek lessons, in which the noble world of classical Greece was brought within the young man's reach. Klee's great love of the Greek classics, which he read in the original nearly every evening before going to sleep, dates from this time, and it was accompanied throughout his life by a similar love of French classical literature. Naturally, his urge to draw was overpowering and the margins of his exercise books were filled with fantastic and often satirical drawings, which, if one can believe Klee's

[1] Strokes of a violinist's bow are meant. (Translator's note.)
[2] He attended the Humanistisches Gymnasium in Bern. (Translator's note.)

23

Concert on a Branch, 1921

school-fellow, anticipated to a great extent much that re-appeared in his later work. In his spare time and during his holidays, however, Paul Klee drew more seriously. First of all Bern and the Elfenau; then Fribourg and Basle, which he visited occasionally; then the Lake of Thun, St. Beatenberg and the Alps made the greatest impressions. And this led Klee to begin drawing landscapes regularly. Some have been pre-served: pages from sketch-books cleanly executed with a well sharpened pencil, drawings in which every plane is clearly marked and the atmospheric qualities of the landscape cap-tured with astonishing accuracy. Towards the objects represented the artist displays remarkable objectivity and the devotion of exact observation. The exact definition of planes taken in conjunction with the pervasive atmospheric tonality, the subtly graded greys united with the affirmative precision of each pencil line, the ordered richness and the perfect balance of these two means, far exceed the dilettantism of a school boy. They already reveal a very genuine preoccupation with the fundamental principles governing the translation of natural images into art. Here the choice between music and the visual arts seems to have been already made.

In September 1898, Paul Klee matriculated, and by October was already on his way to Munich to begin studying art. He presented himself at the Academy but was advised first to attend a private art school. This he did, joining Knirr's school, and on November 15th he could cheerfully report to his great friend in Bern that Knirr had said: 'You have a natural vocation for art. If you work very hard you will achieve something quite exceptional.'

At first Klee did not seem to be over-keen on working hard. The riotous life of the art students and the typical Munich atmosphere were too unfamiliar. But he enjoyed working at Knirr's. He drew busily from models, acquired something of the Munich style, and executed in it several nudes and portraits. Before long he was even able to manage compositions of an idealized and epigrammatic nature, such as were approved of in those days in Munich, where literary painting stood in high favour. Typical subjects were 'Disgust' or 'Shame' or something similar.

The Munich of 1900 was seething with artistic excitement, and two tendencies in particular seemed to point towards a new future. First a lyrical approach to nature, which in the 1890's still promised to develop into a sort of European style of landscape painting. In 1895, painters of the Worpswede school[1] had been awarded gold medals for lyrical pictures of their simple countryside and of the energetic men who tilled it. The school of Worpswede, the Scottish school of Cockburnspath, the followers of the Breton landscape painters: here was a new landscape style evolving from the tradition of the Barbizon painters, which seemed ready to transform painting all over Europe. In Munich, the Dachau painters had early adopted the new ideas,[2] for new ideas were their preoccupation. Here Man found himself responding more deeply, more expressively to nature. Against the simple landscape of heath, wood and moor—primeval forms of landscape—the play of the elements, the wind, the alternation of the seasons and the course of the sun from morning to evening, appeared like new experiences which had to be communicated. Nature in dramatic mood, the dark face of the moor bathed in the glow of the setting sun; or nature in lyric mood, the breath of spring passing rapidly over the birch trees. Such experiences demanded a response from man. All that mattered was expression, the power to put on record the emotion produced by silent happenings of nature. The soul's response, the 'mood' even in the psychic sense, crept imperceptibly into the foreground and forged its own means of expression by formal simplification, monumental composition and intensification of colour. This was a first step towards Expressionist painting. It was very mild, but the ideas out of which Expressionism ultimately grew were evolved here. Nor is it an accident that the first Expressionist painters were nurtured in this artistic climate: Paula Modersohn in the school of Worpswede, Emil

[1] Founded by Fritz Mackensen (b. 1866): other members were Fritz Overbeck, Hans am Ende and Otto Modersohn. Worpswede is in North Germany, near Bremen.
[2] Consisted of Ludwig Dill, Adolf Hölzel, Arthur Langhammer and Karl Langhammer.

Nolde in that of Dachau. The young Paul Klee, too, was affected by this lyrical approach to nature. He, too, began to draw the deserted swampy landscape, and his pictures are full of the melancholy of the dark countryside. He, too, tried his hand at painting massive clumps of trees, which are such a feature of the landscapes of the Dachau school. His drawing became more monumental, his feeling for Nature more romantic and the quiet objectivity of his early drawings yielded to a vague search for expressiveness.

This lyrical approach to nature had a counterpart in the much bolder ideas of certain other artists concerning form, a tendency which I shall here refer to, not entirely accurately, as Jugendstil. These ideas were the subject of heated but inspiring discussions concerning applied art and a stylized form of decoration derived from natural forms, the so-called 'floral style', as well as a non-representational or 'abstract style'. The chief advocate of the 'abstract style' was a Belgian, van de Velde, who exhibited for the first time at the Munich Sezession in 1899. High-sounding phrases were bandied about by both sides in the discussions. They spoke of 'the pure beauty of form', of the expressive power of 'pure line', of 'an art of forms which stirs man's soul through form alone'. We can even read in an article of 1898 by August Endell, that 'we are at the beginning of the development of an entirely new art, the art of forms which mean nothing, represent nothing, and remind us of nothing, but which is able to stir our soul as profoundly and as violently as only music has done hitherto'. In short, the psychic significance of pure line and pure coloured forms had passed into the pictorial thought of the period, despite the repeated emphasis on decoration. So, starting from there, Hoelzel was able, five years later, to draw his first theoretical conclusions concerning the mastery of abstract form, and ten years later Kandinsky was able to paint the first abstract picture. Every intelligent painter during the late 1890's had to come to terms with the two ideological tendencies towards expression and abstraction. Again and again they appeared in the *avant-garde* and most widely read periodicals of the time. Thus there was 'Pan', which first appeared in 1895, 'Die Jugend', from which the whole stylistic tendency took its name, which first appeared in 1896, and 'Simplizissimus', in which the new ideas quickly found additional point when applied to freely drawn caricatures. And the artists had only to look to France to discover similar tendencies in the work of the Pont-Aven school, of the Symbolists and of the Neo-Impressionists. In England, in Belgium, in Scandinavia, everywhere, new movements were afoot, all tending in the same direction. So we must try to imagine how tremendously the young Paul Klee's pictorial thinking was stimulated by these new ideas and how he was inspired to master the magic and mysterious expressive powers of abstract pictorial methods. He was in any case a draughtsman rather than a painter, and line was his means of expression. Now line, with its abstract expressive qualities and its power of psychic communication, was the very element which most interested the *avant-garde* artists of the Jugendstil movement. And when we remember, in addition, Klee's inclination towards the fantastic, the illustrative and the grotesque, we can easily imagine the enthusiasm with which he studied the dreamlike, mystic, sinister drawings of the young Barlach, or of Schmuz-Baudiss, now forgotten, which began to appear in 'Die Jugend' in 1896–7. Some sketches made by Klee at this time, grotesque caricatured heads and illustrative scenes, help us to feel something of his excitement.

However, the profusion of novel ideas in his new surroundings proved rather bewildering and discouraging to Klee, for no sooner had he glimpsed some exciting new perspective than he found it closed again by the teaching of the art-school. At the end of 1899, Klee left Knirr and went to study under Stuck. At last he had joined a real academy. But things do not seem to have gone well for Klee in Stuck's class, and he was not happy. Stuck demanded a thorough knowledge of human anatomy, a demand with which no one was likely to quarrel. But there was no question of being allowed to paint in his class because, curiously enough, Stuck prevented his pupils from using colour, although he himself knew a good deal about it. Furthermore, Klee at this time began to lose confidence in his means of self-expression and toyed with the idea of becoming a sculptor, even making a few first attempts. This was his first spiritual crisis, and it shows that he suffered from considerable disquiet, uncertainty, and the awareness that the form of art then current left him profoundly dissatisfied. Disillusioned, sceptical and confused, he found that he was continually thinking of what radical changes he could effect.

It was in this state of mind that Klee decided on a journey to Italy with his school-friend Hermann Haller, the sculptor. They set off in the late autumn of 1901, and in May 1902 Klee was again in Bern. In all probability Klee's intention in undertaking this journey was to mark the end of his academic studies. The two young men went to Rome, by way of Genoa, visited Naples, and returned home via Florence. Genoa, with its noisy, smelly harbour, the continual movement of shipping, the whiff of far-off Africa and Egypt, and the many different forms of life which thrive under a Southern sun, was a great experience. The sun shone even more brilliantly at Naples, life was mad and enchanted, and the noisy, picturesque, swirling Neapolitan crowd seen in a golden white light reminded him even more of the fabulous enchantment of the East. But Naples had a special experience in store for Klee: the aquarium built by the German zoologist, Dohrn, in connection with his study of submarine life in the Mediterranean. There, behind walls of glass, in a green aqueous light Klee found himself confronted by an unimagined world of forms; objects were visible which no human eye was meant to see. This was a world of forms belonging to another element, deeply concealed natural forms functioning without reference to man. In another, though very familiar, element—water—the world looked different, and in the development of the forms of the sea-urchin, the star-fish, the jelly-fish, the polyp, the sea-anemone and other fishes he was able to discover forms of growth which followed natural laws. Nature was much more complicated, her invention ranged from an elegant, geometrical design of filigree to a strangely contorted play of interlocking forms. This changed everything! The silent creativeness of Nature challenged man's fantasy to indulge in as much freedom. Fantastic and grotesque, nature with its infinite variety of blooms and the ecstatic call of its sexual manifestations, was still richer than man's wildest imaginings. And, underlying everything, there was always a subtle yet strict law of creation according to which these formations developed in themselves and through the generation of their species. This could be guessed, known, but not openly acknowledged. Confronted by such things it is only natural to wish to attain to the same creative freedom, to be aware, all on one's own, of a subtle law which determines the growth of one's own creations. Like Nature! What a task!

But what about art? In Rome, Klee was tremendously impressed by Michael Angelo. He was struck by the controlled pathos of his gesticulating figures, by their overpowering proportions and expressiveness, by his elongated forms, by his immensely accurate knowledge of human anatomy, and by the fact that this knowledge was nevertheless subject to strict control by the pictorial means. All of this sank deep into Klee's

The Beetle, 1925

memory, and its effect was seen in some etchings of figures which he did during the next few years. Then however Michael Angelo receded and early Christian art—mosaics—came to the fore. Could anyone stand before the great mosaic of the Saviour in the Church of SS. Cosmas and Damian in the Forum at Rome and remain unmoved by the abstract beauty of the glowing morning sky behind the majestic figure of the Saviour? Could anyone fail to be moved by the mystery, the immeasurable authority of the gesture and the masterly arrangement of this archaic composition? The glitter of the mosaic tesserae, which impose a sort of abstract filter, gives to the apparition the force of something coming from a world beyond the ken of man, from somewhere indeed where holy people might dwell. These, too, were forceful, abstract things. Then in Florence Klee discovered Gothic art, a special kind of Gothic. As is shown by his etchings of the following years, he must have been captivated by certain artists of c.1400 be' longing to a group which we now call 'international Gothico a style which, in Central Italy, culminated in Fra Angelic-, and in Northern Italy in Pisanello. Here, too, was minuteness and precision at the service of a spiritual vision; an art form in which something naïve, childish and romantic seemed to be drawn like a curtain across the seriousness of the pictorial intention. Klee called the result 'Gothic-classic', and believed that he had caught something of it in his etchings of 1903–6.

But from the human point of view, Klee's journey to Italy marked a decisive turning-point. Klee learnt from it that all his efforts hitherto had led nowhere and could lead nowhere. Art, if it were after all attainable, lay somewhere else. The real outcome as far as he was concerned was thus a profound scepticism about the possibilities of modern art. His reaction took the form of caricatures. And a letter written to his father from Rome on February 2nd 1902, tells of his deep resignation: 'Our art plays a very unimportant role culturally, but that doesn't matter; we came into the world like this and we have to accept it. So, in order not to be laughed at oneself, one gives other people something to laugh at, preferably a picture of themselves. That would be my way of justifying my present efforts.'

32

Klee did not return to Munich. He remained in Bern and settled down there. He had to begin all over again if he was going to win for himself that paradise which he had found in the art of earlier times. Perhaps he would even have to start from the bottom.

Chapter II

YEARS OF APPRENTICESHIP

Everything had to be forgotten. But where to begin? First with man. The important things are human existence, mastery of life, and extension of the horizon, always with an eye to discovering the view-point which has the most meaning. The grass roots of art are not in 'art' alone; they feed on the art of life. In that field one has to trust to fate and let oneself grow like nature. So Klee became conscious that any attempt to over-reach himself, any precocious gesture was a useless and harmful waste of energy. And his belief in letting things grow of their own accord, which frequently meant that he had to wait patiently until the creative image ripened within him, gave him his infallible certainty, his secure feeling of being in the hands of a superior being. He was free from anxiety, and even when the circumstances of his life were unbearably hard, he was able to preserve an inner serenity.

But the gap between one cycle of growth and another had to be filled with work, with frightfully dull work such a-priming canvases, putting on the underpaint, drawing outs lines, arranging forms, putting in highlights, and creating a sense of space with light. All this was connected with the purely pictorial elements of a style; content did not come into play. Klee's early attempts to begin with a poetic idea, his belief that content was the cornerstone of the picture, were false. He had to exchange poetry for construction.

'Wherever I look I see only architecture, linear rhythm, rhythm of planes' he wrote in his diary in 1902. 'Work on the pictorial means begins with the examination of Nature for creative possibilities. Only in this way does one arrive at the first small but personal acts. And while this is going on Nature sometimes opens up and swallows a man. There follows a strange dream, projection of the ego. And out of these more profound experiences comes the revelation that style is the ego. That point is nothingness, *punctum saliens*, the point of genesis. After this, naturally, a glance at the surrounding world compels one to bitter satire, but even this is linked with a glance towards something higher. Satire is not an excess of ill-humour, but ill-humour resulting from a vision of something higher. Ridiculous man—divine God. Hatred of those stuck in the mud out of respect for pure humanity.'

Such were the thoughts that occupied Klee during the year 1902, after his great humiliation in Italy. He plotted the terrain and then saw that what matters is the subjective view of things, their spiritual disposition, their psychic and spiritual enlivenment. Just as classical man had brought the gods down to earth, so modern man had to relegate objects to a remote plane.

But the technical means had to be examined and mastered. Klee drew busily in the anatomy class and in 1903 made a new start with colour, painting nudes and portraits. The result was discouraging. So by way of self-encouragement he turned once again to graphic art and made some etchings. Thus in the summer of 1903 there appeared, in slow succession, his well-known series of etchings 'Woman and Animal', (first state), 'Virgin in a Tree', 'Comedian' (which appeared in three versions) and 'Two men, each imagining the other to be in a superior position, meet'. Their titles are enough to indicate that they are marked by a strong satirical element. They exhibit a rare mixture of the ridiculous and the tragicomic, and it is their ambiguity, half-way between fiction and reality, which gives them their peculiar effect of tragi-comedy. They were not done from life; on the contrary, they caricature and exaggerate nature in the sense of a grotesque super-reality. These figures, carefully modelled, with expressive, almost Gothic gestures, are drawn in a style which is remotely related to Italian 'international Gothic'. Their contemporary stylistic traits are, however, clearly recognizable. In particular, Hodler's influence can be felt; at that time, indeed, everyone around Klee was 'Hodlerizing'. In that same spring, in Zurich, Klee had carefully studied Hodler's *Battle of Marignano*, and from a rapid visit to the Munich Sezession exhibition he had carried away a lasting memory of Hodler's 'William Tell'. If we add to this the stylistic influence of the Vienna Sezession (Klimt), we shall have analysed the contemporary characteristics. Have we gained anything? Everything is so new, so strange; a grotesque super-reality compounded of dream, satire, and a mad, because sham, allegorical secondary meaning. The way from visible to created forms involved a hard struggle through the subsidiary realm of content.

But Klee's pictorial thinking was already ranging further afield. Suddenly he had a vivid recollection of Italian architecture. What was its mysterious secret? Klee noted: the purest expression of the formal principle, the comprehensible relation of one form to another, the clear-cut independent organism, the 'visibly calculable relation of one part to another and to the whole which corresponds to hidden numerical relationships in other artificial and natural organisms'. Everything is based upon numbers, relationships which are the breath of life. Measurement is all-important. These little hidden numbers also govern the endlessly complicated forms of Nature. A knowledge of Nature is not just a matter of being familiar with the apparent forms of its ultimate ramifications; on the contrary, it depends on gaining an insight by formal means into those ultimate ramifications and seeing that they 'provide us with precise analogies for the entire code of laws'. This was a profound vision, and it implied an attempt to find a common formal root for both art and Nature.

Already therefore Klee had the desire to experience the world as a whole: he did not wish to dwell on isolated examples, either in Nature, or in man. He found himself thinking, very much like Kleist, that the two bright peaks of knowledge are those of animals and of Gods, the one a paradisiac unawareness, the other the purest awareness of divinity. Between them, in a dark valley, stands man, longing to attain to both these peaks within himself, to achieve harmony, to discover the circle of the whole, to see, as Kleist says: 'Whether perhaps the back door of Paradise is open again.'

But it is difficult to set all this in motion. Klee spent the year 1904 constantly experimenting. His difficulty was to combine study of Nature with respect for pure form. Sometimes he achieved what he wanted with a few nervous penstrokes which seemed to be full of expression, and then he had the idea of relying more on accidents of line for spontaneity and originality. Rodin's drawings of nudes provided him with an example of the spontaneous descriptive properties of line. But Klee felt that it was still too early for him to abandon the conception of form and the severe style of his early etchings.

So in the summer of 1904 he made two more etchings, 'Female Grace' and 'Allegory of the Mountain'; and towards the end of that year he made the second version of 'Woman and Animal', the 'Monarchist', and the 'New Perseus'. Restless and dissatisfied, Klee felt obliged in the autumn to go to Munich. There, in the Print Room, he looked at works by Beardsley and was puzzled. Blake on the other hand he fully understood, and he was enthusiastic about Goya's 'Proverbios', 'Caprichos' and 'Desastros de la Guerra'.

Goya was uppermost in Klee's mind at the beginning of 1905, and during the first few months he continued to work on his series of engravings. He produced the 'Hero with a Wing', the 'Aged Phoenix', and 'Menacing Head', which was intentionally the last. And that was the end of Klee's work in this severe super-realistic style. Klee felt satisfied, for he found his work honest and sincere; but there was something new within himself which was determined to find expression. Goya gave him no peace. Goya represented, at one and the same time, an artist who remained true to himself in transcribing his spontaneous vision, but whose control of tonal values was so exact that he could obtain the maximum of dramatic tension simply in black and white. Next, therefore, Klee had to master the realm of tonal values. And at that stage Klee made a discovery, while searching, as usual, for the appropriate technique to apply to some other pictorial problem. He blackened a pane of glass and scratched on it with a needle. His line then appeared as white energy against a dark ground. And this corresponded with what he had seen in Nature, whose forms are made visible by rays of light. So Klee started to replace the black abstraction of line by a light-medium which produced a similar effect, and this led him quite naturally towards the new realm of tonal values. It was just like

WATERCOLOUR PAINTED ON GLASS, 1907
Collection F. Laurens, Cincinnati

THE NIESEN, 1915
Private Collection, Bern (Rupf)

Nature. As it evolved, the white line immediately took on a temporal character; its effect developed genetically. Then the parallel with music, which also exists temporally, suggested itself.

Tonality, light and adaptability of the means—anyone who has reached that point stands on the threshold of Impressionism. In June, Klee and a friend, the Swiss painter Louis Moilliet, went to Paris for a few days. But once again, it was Goya who made the greatest impression on Klee. Indeed, he began to distrust the doctrine of 'L'art pour l'Art', and took as his credo instead the saying of Oscar Wilde that 'all art is simultaneously surface and symbol'. Now a symbol has a more precise significance the more the spiritual and psychic impulses inherent in its lines point towards another and higher dimension. After that came the question of objects in general. Klee thought he saw clearly that objects in themselves no longer mattered, and that it was more his reactions to objects which wanted to find expression. This conception implied a freer conception of form and enabled the artist to reproduce with greater mobility the range of his inner emotions. Thereafter he could envisage transmitting psychographic values by means of line, while handling forms somewhat automatically. But there remained Nature, that complex of Man and Nature, which cannot be encompassed by psychography and automatism. So Klee concluded: 'It is all a matter of the law according to which Nature functions and of how it sometimes reveals itself to the artist.'

Klee now began to feel more sure of himself, as he thought he could perceive whither his slow and steady growth was leading. The immediate aim seemed to be to let his own personality speak. In June 1906, he wrote to his fiancée: 'With all possible simplicity and artistic licence I am attempting to pin down every expression of my soul.' But that can only be accomplished by pictorial construction, not by illustration of poetic or allegorical subjects. So Klee was only satisfied with the result when 'a poetic and a pictorial thought happen to correspond'. He spent the whole of the year 1906 painting on glass and experimenting with related techniques. At the same time great changes occurred in Klee's personal life. In October he married Lili Stumpf, a pianist who was a few years older than himself, and the two of them moved to Munich. There, in a modest dwelling—Ainmillerstrasse 32, Gartenhaus, 2nd floor, right—Klee set up house. He had no studio except the kitchen. But he worked, did the modest housekeeping and cooked lovely Italian food, because his wife had to earn the money for the household by giving music lessons. In November 1907 their number was increased by the birth of a son, Felix. In spite of poverty, it was a grand life, plenty of concerts, plenty of music at home, and Klee felt certain that something in himself was growing steadily and consistently. At last he could sort out the many exciting artistic experiences he had known in Munich. Klee was interested by Pascin's drawings in '*Simplizissimus*', by his fine, nervous, but pre-eminently graphic line; he was even more impressed by the fantasy of James Ensor, whose graphic *oeuvre* he came to know in the autumn of 1907. Here again Klee found a fantastic super-reality and mysterious communications from an inner self profoundly buried in the rhythm of the linear network. The significance for Klee of the years 1906–7 was exactly that of letting things develop out of himself. He had control over line, and an insight into the world of tonalities. He had not, however, reconciled the world without and the world within. This was a fusion which had to be attained. An intensified study of nature, resulting in a series of landscapes painted in black and white on glass, occupied him during the summer of 1907. These were intended to narrow the gap. In his determination to effect a reconciliation Klee even considered arbitrary distortions of nature. But he had to learn to be patient. The problem as he saw it was clear: how to enjoy the greatest freedom in building a bridge between the world within and the world without. 'Oh, delicious line of the arc of this bridge—patience, my soul!'

The year 1908 was of great importance, for then Klee first saw pictures by Van Gogh at two exhibitions in private galleries in Munich. Klee had already seen some modern French painting—Bonnard, Vuillard, Valloton—at the Spring Salon, but he did not feel very enthusiastic about it. Van Gogh was quite different. Klee had a profound human understanding of Van Gogh's 'representative tragedy'. But because he understood him so profoundly, he shrank from the pathological aspect of this all-consuming genius. Yet, for the sake of his own evolution, Klee now needed Van Gogh to help him to develop visions such as Ensor had opened up for him. Van Gogh's ability to transcend naturalism depends on the fact that he treated line as an independent pictorial element. Form as an independent element; therein lay for Klee the new freedom.

In March 1908, Klee produced a really valid, if small, black and white picture on glass, 'The Balcony'. This is a view through the curving ironwork of a balcony outside his kitchen on to an open plot of ground, beyond which is a busy city street. Here Klee succeeded in transposing the accidental qualities of a slice of nature into a highly simplified type, at the same time preserving the purity of the linear and tonal (black-white progression) elements, and developing the one genetically out of the other. This study of tonal-values in Nature led of its own accord to a constructive figuration. As one layer of grey, getting gradually darker, was superimposed on another until maximum depth was attained, an exact proportion developed out of the sum of the carefully graded grey tones. The picture grew genetically from layer to layer within the proportions of this light-dark relationship. A correspondence was established between the natural and the constructional elements. That was indeed Klee's first concern: to reconcile Nature and his picture. Here, too, Klee devised for himself an aid to composition. He drew faithfully from Nature then turned his sheet of paper upside down and decided in the abstract on the form of the construction he was going to make. Then he turned the sheet of paper round again and proceeded to reconcile his construction with Nature.

Construction. That is the real basis of a picture, its scaffolding, its skeleton, its physical body. And it has its own anatomy. Every step in picture-making is abstract and tectonic, it adds to the scaffolding around which the body of the picture takes form genetically. 'How far one goes beyond this scaffolding is optional; the scaffolding can exert itself as art and create a deeper effect than that caused by the surface alone.' But at the bottom of everything, even though one cannot say exactly how and where, are the creative processes of Nature. Even light, the most dynamic element in Nature, assumes a material form as one constructional element is played off against another: curves are made straight, straight lines become curved, empty spaces are filled with movement, and light assumes shapes of its own in these empty spaces. And through the movement of these constructive forms the psychological element takes on a greater emphasis. For although the construction of a pure formal entity is already a considerable achievement, it is not everything. Content too is important. This preoccupation with a pure handling of line,

DEMON OVER THE BOATS, 1916
Museum of Modern Art, New York

MILDLY TROPICAL LANDSCAPE, 1918
Private Collection, Stuttgart

of tonality and of form was intended to bring Klee back to the real issue which he described as his 'original province of psychic improvisation'. 'I can dare to depict what weighs upon my soul in an image which is only very indirectly related to an impression of Nature. Make notes of experiences which could be transposed into line even in the dark. In this way my pure personality can be most freely liberated.'

Construction and psychic improvisation: this is an adequate basis for self-realization where the logical workings of pictorial thinking are concerned. A picture is begun as a construction; its immutable expression is then provided by coloured forms grouped according to the free sensibility of the artist. He then sets about interpreting the objective content of this free image —Klee was reminded here of how in extreme youth he had seen imaginary pictures in the veins of the marble-topped tables—bringing it to the fore and giving the content of the picture concrete form on the psychic plane. There was salvation in this idea. At first it presents itself unexpectedly, naked as something newborn, at the beginning of a new species of pictures. That is why I said earlier that the year 1908 was very important. For in the ideas which I have outlined we can discover in embryo the vision which runs through the whole of Klee's work. And by comparison with the ideas the results are often unimportant, because during these years of apprenticeship Klee was not concerned with results, but with the direction he was following and with the consolidation of his progress towards an ultimate flowering of results.

Klee was not in search of results but of discipline; and in the face of Nature his pictorial discipline led him to reduce the scale of his pictures. The only way to say more than Nature is to use fewer means. 'If my things sometimes produce a primitive impression, the explanation of this "primitiveness" lies in my discipline of reducing everything to a small number of steps. It is simply economy, that is to say the last professional lesson.' Klee spent the year 1909 attempting to har-

An Alarming Moment, 1912

monize general tonalities and areas of colour, letting them combine to form images. And at the same time he studied nature eagerly in order to gather forms which he could then elaborate. But something else of importance happened this year: at the Spring Salon Klee saw for the first time a picture by Cézanne. At once (and no sentimentality was involved) Klee understood that in Cézanne he had found his true master, for in his own way Cézanne had succeeded in providing a bridge between Nature and his picture, between the world within and the world without. He thus became a magnificent inspiration.

In 1910, inspired by Cézanne's example, Klee turned with greater determination to the new and fundamental problem of colour. He tried at first to use colours as he had previously used black and white in his water-colours—that is to say classifying the tonal values as various shades of grey and piling them up as the picture progressed. Thus in place of graduated tonal values he substituted a sliding scale of colour. But he found that he still could not achieve all that he wanted. So once again he tried to solve the problem by purely pictorial means. He made the 'revolutionary discovery', that the artist's attitude to the colours in his paint-box is more important than studying Nature. In consequence he resolved that one day he would possess the freedom to improvise chromatically over the full range of his palette. First of all he tried to impose all that he knew about drawing on the domain of colour. That is to say he would begin a picture by using colour in a quite abstract way, arranging areas of colour according to the degree of his emotion, then imposing an independent drawing on top of this coloured construction, and finally consolidating any weaknesses resulting from this duality by additional notes of colour.

From this year date Klee's first small successes. He held an exhibition of his prints and drawings in Switzerland, and towards the end of the year had the satisfaction of being approached by Kubin, who expressed admiration for his work, talked of 'the neighbourly relationship' between their aims and asked Klee to make him a present of a drawing.

In January 1911, Kubin came in person to see Klee. His praise was extravagant, but Klee remained calm. The relationship between Klee and Kubin is generally misinterpreted. Klee has nothing to do with Kubin. Admittedly Klee was struck by the sensitive and expressive character of Kubin's line, which he used to reveal, in purely pictorial terms, a fantastic world of his own. But with Kubin that remained rudimentary. 'He got stuck half-way, longed for the crystalline essence, but could never extract himself from the quicksands of the world of appearances,' Klee wrote in his diary of 1915. Probably both of them started from a fundamentally similar conception. But whereas Kubin only dreamt about the possibilities of line as a means, Klee was already at work making it come true on the pictorial plane. This sounds incredible, yet it can be proved. In Kubin's novel *Die Andere Seite* (*The Other Side*) written and published in 1908–9, it is possible to find passages which correspond exactly with Klee's thought. The narrator of the novel describes how: 'For hours on end I now tried to contemplate stones, flowers, animals and men in the mass. In this way my eye was sharpened. The more I trained my senses the more they gradually influenced my thought processes and transformed them. I became capable of a surprising kind of astonishment. Objects ripped out of their context among other objects acquired a new significance. It made me shudder to think that a body seized thus from oblivion could make contact with myself. One day, when I was looking at a shell, it became appallingly clear to me that its existence was not as trivial as I had formerly believed. Somehow one had gradually to create a world that is not necessarily alive, and indeed create it anew. More and more, I felt that there is a common bond between everything. And then I knew: the world is the power of imagination, imagination—power.' This imaginary painter then sees the world from his somewhat extra-human point of view in quite another way. 'Once I saw the world as a tapestry-like miracle of colour, in which the most amazing contrasts were resolved in a harmony; another time I found myself surveying an immeasurable filigree of forms. Like a sleep-walker, I found myself reacting to quite new sensations. I remember a particular morning when I felt that I was the centre of an elementary system of numbers. I felt that I was abstract, like the balancing point between two competing forces.' There follows the transformation of all these experiences into abstract pictorial terms. 'A series of little works was produced. In these I tried to create new and direct images based on secret rhythms of which I had become conscious; they writhed, got entangled, and exploded against each other. I went still further. I renounced everything except line, and during these months evolved a peculiar system of lines. It was a fragmentary style, writing rather than drawing, but like a sensitive meteorological instrument it recorded even the slightest oscillations of my inner mood. "Psychography" was the name I gave to this procedure.' So much for Kubin's daydreams. But in his actual drawings he stuck closely to subject-matter and tried to express his wildest fantasies as nearly as possible in terms of objects. Indeed, one might say that in origin the pictorial thinking of Kubin and Klee was identical, but that Klee took latent thoughts and tried to make them concrete by the pictorial means of drawing.

In 1911, drawing was once again foremost among Klee's interests. Consequently, also Van Gogh. What fascinated Klee was that Van Gogh had found an expressive line 'which made use of Impressionism and at the same time went beyond it'. 'In my case', Klee noted in his diary, 'this helped me to solve the divergence between my erratic scribbling and firmly drawn contours, and it is going to help me to attain something else still—a line which eats up and digests the scribbles. Assimilation. The surfaces still look rather bare, but this won't last long.' In the spring of this year, Klee began a series of some thirty illustrative drawings for Voltaire's *Candide*. Klee, who was a great reader, discovered this book in 1906

Illustration for Voltaire's 'Candide', 1911

and it made an unusually deep impression on him. The tragi-comedy of Candide, a sort of 'pure fool' so to speak, who, in spite of all the meanness and adversity of life, is not prepared to renounce his faith in the best of all worlds, fitted Klee's mood perfectly. As he wrote later: 'Were I God, I would found an order whose banner consisted of tears doing a gay dance.' In 1905 Klee had produced his 'Hero with a Wing', a 'hero specially conceived by nature with only one wing, who nevertheless had the idea that he was intended to fly, and so came to grief'. *Candide* is a supremely sarcastic description of this sort of tragi-comic situation, written with all the precision and economy of which the French language is capable. This gave Klee no rest. In 1909 already he had longed to do these illustrations, but his preoccupation with colour and the impression made on him by Cézanne had prevented him thinking about such things as illustrative line drawings.

Klee's renewed preoccupation with Van Gogh, and his prolonged work on the cultivation of pure line, had however prepared the way for him to do something of his own. Drawings like these had never been seen before. Thin, scratchy lines seem to encompass rather than define interminably elongated figures with tiny heads. They set up a sort of atmospheric vibration which is something between a vague reflection and an indistinct reality. It is as though a series of fleeting images were materializing in some fluctuating medium; they get caught at a level where nothing visible is reproduced. The web of lines is made entirely by the expressive movements of the artist's hand; it is an expressive tracery whose abstract course only materializes in figurative gesticulation. It corresponds exactly to what Klee called a 'psychic improvisation', and on the graphic plane completes the bridge which he had been looking for between the world within and the world without, because it is simultaneously psychic improvisation and illustrative description. Here Klee completed the first stage of something that he was then free to develop: a form of graphic art developing out of the expressive movements of his hand.

This led Klee to turn his attention towards certain fundamental psychic states of man in which 'psychic improvisation' is still taken for granted. He looked more closely at the drawings of children (the first attempts at painting of his young son Felix offered welcome material) and of madmen. These

D   49

elementary beginnings of art, he thought, should be taken seriously, 'more seriously than many a museum if we are really set on reforming things to-day'. Klee's attitude to the art of children, about which we have heard such a lot, was clear. To him it was the most primitive form of art; therefore he was interested purely and simply in discovering how a primitive instinct finds a formal structure appropriate to content. For children, as opposed to artists, are concerned with nothing else. Klee was thus studying the formative powers of the unconscious; however, a child, who is entirely pre-occupied with mastering visible objects, has no time to think about such things. And Klee turned all his powers of analysis on to studying the growth of formal images from their simplest pictorial starting point.

Klee was gradually emerging from his years of apprenticeship and beginning to see results. Then for the first time, after working for many years on his own, he established contact with artists of similar aims. Kubin re-visited him, and in the summer Klee joined the newly founded 'Sema' (The Sign) group of artists, to which Caspar, Oppenheimer and Scharff as well as Kubin belonged. That was an event of no consequence, but his meeting with the members of the 'Blaue Reiter' was important.

Chapter III

THE EUROPEAN PHALANX

In the autumn of 1911 Klee became acquainted with Kandinsky through his friend Louis Moilliet. The two painters quickly developed an interest in each other's work and before Christmas Klee had joined the 'Blaue Reiter'.

The Blaue Reiter! That meant a wonderful world full of impulses and power! The artistic daring of Kandinsky, with his rich Asiatic heritage, knew no bounds, and his was a truly revolutionary talent. His forms were irradiated by strong colours, and objects were dissolved. Objective details were still to be found here and there in his pictures of this time—an angel with a trumpet, a galloping *troïka*, the golden domes of Moscow—but they had no more value than as hieroglyphs, hints at a theme which was swallowed up by the resonant harmonies of coloured forms, which ran from white and light yellow at the top of the scale down to purple and dark blue at the bottom. Like Russian choral music, rising abnormally high, and falling abnormally deep. Yet it was a new intellectually controlled system of tonalities. And the essential feature of these pictures was not so much the constructive play of one coloured form against another, nor yet the transformation of something visible into an independent pictorial fact, but an overpowering subjective feeling orchestrated with coloured forms. They were a deliberate demonstration that our inner emotions can be visually conveyed in a picture entirely by means of the expressive properties of colour and the psychographic properties of arabesques. They were complemented by the priest-like Gothic dreams of Franz Marc, whose deep love of creation was such that it could change the world into a pictorial parable, a parable of the deep harmony prevailing among all living things in the world around him. And the solemn hierarchy of Marc's forms is an expression of the profound longing for a harmonious existence which is common to everything in this world. That is to say these are devotional images which express a pantheistic religious emotion. Next came the bright, colourful world of August Macke, nature joyfully comprehended. Macke looked with delight at nature decked out in all her beauty until she became transparent and yielded up the secret of her web of poetic colour. Then he saw this beauty existing independently: the world as a coloured legend.

Kandinsky, Marc, Macke—these were the three painters of the 'Blaue Reiter', beside whom Klee took his place. He met Kandinsky in the autumn of 1911. He had met August Macke earlier that same summer at Moilliet's, but it was not until the late summer of 1912 that he met Marc. All four artists were concerned with the spiritual side of art. And their common task, which Klee also felt that he must face, was to transform Nature into a visual equivalent of what we imagine it to be. The pictorial realization of the dreams which haunt us expressed as an artistic construction. Transformation and realization! It all happened because of a deep inner necessity, because the conventional world was no longer bearable and everything threatened to suffocate in weariness and lies. As

THE EUROPEAN PHALANX

Franz Marc wrote in 1912: 'The world is full to suffocation. Man has deposited a pledge of his cleverness on every stone. Every word is hired or borrowed. What can one do to attain happiness except give up everything and escape? Or perhaps draw a line between yesterday and to-day?' This outburst left a deep scar. But the task of these reformers was not to conceal the scar, but to keep the wound open and explore the area themselves. Klee responded warmly to this task. For, just before the first exhibition of the 'Blaue Reiter' (which opened in December, though Klee did not take part) he had reached the conclusion that here, too, he was getting to the newly-discovered basis of all art, to the 'primitive origins of art'. And whilst Klee looked for these 'primitive origins' in children's drawings, ethnographical objects and folk art, Kandinsky discovered Bavarian peasant paintings on glass. Picasso, Matisse and Braque were collecting negro masks in the junk shops of Paris, but Franz Marc was spellbound by African and Inca sculptures in the Berlin Ethnographical Museum. On the 14th January 1911, Marc wrote to Macke about his experience: 'We must be brave and turn our back on almost everything that until now good Europeans like ourselves have thought precious and indispensable. Our ideas and ideals must be clad in hair-shirts, they must be fed on locusts and wild honey, not on history, if we are ever to escape from the exhaustion of our European bad taste.' But Klee had already made a remarkable entry in his diary in 1902: 'I want to be as though new-born, knowing nothing about Europe, nothing, knowing no pictures, entirely without impulses, almost in an original state.' Klee now found a similar concern with the origins of art among his fellow-artists of the 'Blaue Reiter'. Their pictures would have no imitative purpose. They had to evolve a language of forms and colours in order that messages could be transmitted from the new dimension of the world of expression within man.

In the opinion of the others, Klee perhaps did not count for much. He was more of a moral support than a performer, for he was not yet quite ready, he had still not mastered the problem of colour (Kandinsky was to be of assistance to him over this). They were wrestling with works of large dimensions and for that reason can be excused if they tended to overlook Klee's microcosm. At any rate, Klee's name is never mentioned in connection with artistic matters in the whole of the long correspondence between Marc and Macke. They were all close friends and saw each other frequently. Indeed the Marcs regarded the Klees as their closest friends, but when Klee's name was mentioned, it was always primarily in connection with music and with the pleasure derived from listening to Mozart, Beethoven, Bach, Handel or Cesar Franck, played by Klee on the violin. Marc and Kandinsky liked Klee's drawings very much. It was Marc who suggested to the publisher Piper that he should do an edition of *Candide* illustrated with Klee's drawings; he also insisted that Herwarth Walden should reproduce drawings by Klee both inside and on the cover of *Der Sturm*. In the second 'Blaue Reiter' exhibition of prints and drawings, which was held in the upper rooms of the Goltz gallery in Munich in March 1912, Klee was represented. But Klee never played a leading role in the 'Blaue Reiter'. He was not even represented at the famous Sonderbund exhibition of 1912. But that did not matter to him. The 'Blaue Reiter' meant freedom for Klee; he had reached a point from which he could look deep into the domain of free form and free colour.

Klee's field of vision now took in things happening elsewhere in Europe. As early as September 1910 the Neue

Künstlervereinigung (a group originally formed by Kandinsky; the 'Blaue Reiter' broke away from this in 1911) had invited French artists to exhibit with them, especially the young painters of the Fauve movement, Le Fauconnier, Derain, Vlaminck, and Rouault, but also the Cubists, Braque and Picasso. The first 'Blaue Reiter' exhibition included pictures by Henri Rousseau and Robert Delaunay; and its exhibitions of prints and drawings included work by Braque, Derain, de la Fresnaye, Picasso and Vlaminck. Goltz was the first dealer in Munich to exhibit Cubist pictures by Braque, Derain and Picasso in his shop-window, and here and there in exhibitions Klee saw other pointers towards freedom. So Klee felt the urge to look around in Paris for himself, and he set off there for a fortnight at the beginning of April 1912. At Uhde's and at Kahnweiler's he saw the new Parisian masters in all their asceticism and richness—Braque, Picasso, Derain, Rousseau. Matisse he saw at Bernheim's; Delaunay he visited in his studio. These were new and deeply moving impressions, the most important of which was his contact with Cubism. And it seems to have been the severe formal constructions of Georges Braque with their subtle harmonies of grey, yellow and brown which impressed Klee most profoundly.

Starting from Cézanne's spatial and surface abstractions, the Cubists treated their pictures as independent formal organisms and only made use of natural objects as abstract elements of form. The first step was to transform a three-dimensional object into a formal element within the two-dimensional domain of the picture. But at the same time its full physical reality and normal proportions had to be recognizably preserved. Picasso once said: 'In a picture by Raphael, it is impossible to determine the distance from the tip of the nose to the mouth. I should like to paint pictures in which this would be possible.' So the Cubists began to analyse and dissect objects, painting simultaneous views of them from the front, from above, and from the side, and amalgamating the result into an independent formal structure which was nevertheless a description of the original object. Every system of classification devised by man shows a similar concern with numbers and proportions, with geometrical elements. In Cubist pictures too we see how objects can be turned into geometrical forms, into those spheres, cones and cubes which, as Cézanne said, are the basic forms of Nature. Now if objects were to be subordinated to a rigid process of abstract classification, the same procedure had to be applied to pictorial space. Pictures had to cease being windows through which one looks into an illusory naturalistic space. Pictorial space had to become independent. So the Cubists limited space in their pictures with a rigid background from which the forms come forward in successive spatial planes as in a bas-relief. Each picture produced its own sense of space by a series of planes related to the plane of the canvas within which the hierarchy of pictorial values is built up and arranged. Into this independent pictorial organism the Cubist painter would then insert 'real' objects—newspaper cuttings for example, if he was painting a still-life with a newspaper, letters of the alphabet, wall-paper and so. These 'real' objects have the effect of quotations, recalling to the spectator's mind memories of actual objects, thus helping him to read the picture and to recognize a particular object within the free rhythmical unity of the picture. Objects which the spectator has thus recognized by association then take on their full spatial reality in his mind, are experienced as though recreated genetically. Hence they can be seen afresh with a penetration which cannot be achieved in illusionistic art. Ideas such as these had been in

Klee's mind for a long while; suddenly he found them realized with logic in the formal constructions of the French.

Here the gap between the world within and the world without had been bridged, at least in the case of the limited problem of objects. This was both abstract and at the same time representational art, an artistic idiom which ensured two possibilities for a picture—to be a reflection of Nature and a lyrical equivalent of a human mood. For Klee, Cubism signified the artist's complete freedom to choose his own forms provided that he respected the strict laws of picture-making.

Then, however, he came across Robert Delaunay, a figure of great importance to Klee. *Peinture pure* was the new conception that Delaunay had made essentially his own, and the poet Apollinaire wrote about it in *Der Sturm* in 1912. Colour, light, movement—such were the elements with which Delaunay's mind played. Each had to be assured of independent significance. And Delaunay explained: 'Our eyes are sensitive in order that we shall see that there are colours, that colours represent modulations, monumental relationships, depths, vibrations, playfulness, that colours breathe. . . . No more Eiffel Towers, street scenes, visible world. . . . The apples are no longer in the bowl; the heartbeat of man himself is there instead.' In 1913 there appeared in *Der Sturm* an article on light by Delaunay translated by Klee, from which I would like to quote some passages. 'Nature is permeated by a multiplicity of rhythms which admit of no restraint,' wrote Delaunay. 'Art imitates her in this respect, then attains a similar grandeur by clarification, taking on the appearance of manifold harmonies, harmonies of colour which separate and re-unite into a whole in a single action. This synchronized action is the only true subject of painting.' The same applies to light. 'So long as art is subservient to objects, it remains description,

57

literature, and degrades itself by relying on defective means of expression. This is also true when the intention is to depict the luminous appearance of an object or the light-relationships between several objects, unless at the same time light is treated as an independent means of representation.' Delaunay then made the discovery, in terms of light and colour, of space-time and movement, a discovery which Klee had already made with line. Delaunay spoke of the *simultanéisme* of colour, of its *sens giratoire*, meaning by this the suggestions of movement which emanate from the concerted action of several colours, and give the picture an additional space-time dimension, the *forme-espace* which is completed by the *forme-temps*, as Gleizes later called it. 'A figure in motion can be caught with the universal language of colour,' asserted Delaunay. Now these were problems to which Klee had already devoted himself in his graphic work; here he found them being tackled in the domain of colour. Admittedly Kandinsky too had spoken of the abstract significance and relationship of colours, but he had never really faced up to their spatial function. Compared with that of Delaunay, Kandinsky's painting at this time was chaotic; his pictures were visions in which the cosmos was reflected, but he did not know exactly how to represent the space within which his picture was situated. Kandinsky's pictorial space was thoroughly illusionistic; a section of space so to speak. But, in his Eiffel Tower pictures and in his Cubist phase, Delaunay had fully explored the possibilities of pictorial space and had arrived at a form of independent pictorial space in which the play of colours could function with precision. Klee could appreciate this. And if we attach any importance to establishing a source for his art, then we must assign the major share to 'Orphic Cubism', as the movement associated with Delaunay has been called.

At this point Klee was exposed to a new experience from an unexpected quarter, from Italy. In the late autumn of 1912 Herwarth Walden, the founder of *Der Sturm*, exhibited pictures by the Italian Futurists—Carrà, Boccioni, Severini, and Russolo—at the Thannhauser Gallery in Munich. They were enthusiastically received by the 'Blaue Reiter'. Franz Marc wrote in *Der Sturm* in October 1912: 'Carrà, Boccioni and Severini will become landmarks in the history of modern painting. We shall yet envy Italy her sons and hang their works in our galleries.' But Klee found himself combining the ideas of the Futurists with those of Delaunay which had so excited him. What were the ideas of the Futurists? First of all an enthusiastic acceptance of the facts of modern life, of the rhythm of great cities, of the aesthetic of the machine and of speed as the absolute essence of modernity. The fundamental Futurist sensation of modern civilization was dynamism, 'the violent explosions of movement and of speed, the intoxication of action'. So they introduced entirely new pictorial themes such as: 'The Noise of the Street penetrates into the Room', 'The Jolting Tram', 'The Express Train', 'The Funeral of the Anarchist', etc. The method adopted by the Futurists to express such themes consisted of packing into a picture, as a complex unity, all the simultaneous aspects of reality. The surrounding world penetrates directly into the existence of an object, permeates it, completes it, and deforms it. The catalogue of the Futurist Exhibition of 1912, held first in Berlin then in Munich, stated: 'It is absurd and a spiritual betrayal to copy directly from a model. We must also express the invisible, that which moves and has its being on the other side of a static object, that which is to the right and left of us and behind us. We cannot be content with a little square of life which is artifically enclosed like the stage of a theatre.' For the

Futurists, movement had two aspects: (1) *Absolute* movement, that is to say, dynamic lines indicating how an object would disintegrate in accordance with the nature of its inherent formal forces. This can be expressed in dynamic abstract forms. (2) *Relative* movement, that is to say the actual movement of the object itself. 'A moving horse is not a stationary horse, but a horse in motion; that is quite a different thing, and must also be expressed as a different thing.' So for everything in motion, that is to say for life itself in so far as we regard it as action, we must discover the appropriate dynamic formula by which it can be represented. Dynamism is the integration of the formal motive tendencies of an object with the representational formula of its actual movement in its surroundings. The Futurists expressed this in the formula: surroundings plus object.

The representational means for expressing this formula is 'simultaneity', the simultaneous representation of all the sensations contained in a given *motif*. According to the Futurists, a passive representation of a woman at a window, for example, had none of the sensations which are peculiar to the theme. And the Futurists meant by these sensations the noise of the street, the clanging of a passing tram, the busy movement of life going on below the window with their effect upon the mood and the memory of the woman. A picture therefore should be an artistic formula which catches the whole of this complex reality. Individual planes of reality—inside and outside, far and near, things seen and things imagined—are interpenetrating, being simultaneously represented on the canvas and forged by the artist's intuition into a new unity. The task of the Futurist artist was to construct a complex new reality, for which objects of the outer world provide pictorial analogies. Futurism is, therefore, a pictorial theory which attempts to represent an experience of reality in its entirety by allowing the pictorial signs for things seen to become confused with pictorial signs for things known, heard, felt or remembered, the whole being set in motion by lines of dynamic force extracted from the inherent motive tendencies of objects.

Klee found in such ideas a welcome confirmation of his own thoughts. Delaunay, the Cubists, and the Futurists—there he had solid foundations on which to build. Klee saw at once that a rich new territory had been added to the domain of art. Formally, he found Carrà the most interesting. But what amazed him most was to find that he could now represent those themes which interested him especially, themes such as those announced in the Futurist manifesto: 'When one opens a window, all the noise of the street, the movement and the objectivity of things outside suddenly enter the room.' Or more far-reaching still: 'The force of the street, the life, the ambition, the anxiety that one can observe in a great city, the feeling of oppression caused by the noise.' And just as Marc felt that the Futurists were completely successful in painting and expressing such things, so Klee felt that he saw them most 'convincingly represented' in the Futurist Exhibition.

In his review of the exhibition Franz Marc noted that, from the standpoint of French *belle peinture*, the pictures of the Futurists might well be criticized. But was that the point? Not to him, and not to Klee. There was a great deal of discussion about this at the time between Marc, Klee and Macke. For Macke was very much on the side of French *belle peinture*, particularly after 1913; and his belief in Matisse and Delaunay led him to break with Kandinsky. Not so Klee and Marc, and we are given an insight into their point of view in a letter from Marc to Macke of 12th June 1914. 'I tend to agree with Klee', Marc wrote, 'whose opinion you will have heard. I am a German and can only dig my own plot of ground. What does the *peinture* of the Orphists matter to me? We Germans are and always will be born draughtsmen, illustrators, even when we are painters.' This is rather crudely expressed. Klee's view probably was that, above and behind the formal composition and the aesthetically pleasing surface harmonies of a picture, there must be another precious element which leads to the dimension of content and thus to the revelation of a message. The themes of the Futurists, which always had something materialistic about them, could be developed much further on the psychic plane. The process of 'psychic improvisation' should enable him to call up remote and quite unusual things, poetic themes from every psychic level from the sublime to the grotesque. These he could make visible with the means of 'simultaneity', free lines, free form, free colour and dynamic motive impulses. For a while longer Klee remained predominantly a graphic artist, for he needed first of all to absorb the new conceptions of the Cubists and Futurists and evolve an idiom which he could handle with confidence. But even so the moment did not pass without a communication from the endless repertory of expressive human themes. 'Garden of Passion' was the title of his new etching, 'Suicide on a Bridge' that of a drawing. These are highly polished, small-scale, almost abstract works, like puzzle pictures, with strong motive impulses and themes derived from the psychic dimension. 'I am now able to express these and similar things with some poignancy,' Klee wrote in his diary at the end of 1913, 'and this by line alone, by line as an absolute spiritual element with no analytical function. This is simply a foretaste.'

Chapter IV

THE GIFT OF COLOUR

Simply a foretaste! Klee had taken stock of the domain of colour but he had not yet begun to cultivate it. Before he could attempt this Klee needed an overwhelming optical experience. It came, and the full extent of his experience is to be seen in many pictures of the next few years. So let us examine one of these pictures.

The picture I have chosen is neither signed nor dated. The label of the 'Sturm' Gallery[1] is stuck on the back, and this tells us that the title is 'Mildly Tropical Landscape' and that its date is 1918. It is an ensemble of very mobile forms held together in a crystalline balance. The coloured forms, clearly defined and for the most part abstract and geometrical, are arranged in layers within the picture-space, which enjoys an independent existence spatially and has no perspective. It is an abstract formal organism of great beauty which exists in and for itself. The dominant colours are a radiant blue, terracotta, yellow and green. The colour structure advances by layers towards the foreground plane. Dark blue provides a radiant background—dark light; in front of it are layers of terracotta, which turn orange as they advance to the front, and in so doing push a light yellow and a green triumphantly

[1] An art gallery in Berlin founded by Herwarth Walden.

63

into the foreground. As we lose ourselves in this radiant crystal we gradually become aware of familiar forms. In the foreground—the growing force of the yellow already leads us to talk of a foreground—we see a fat plant growing out of a yellow sandhill; nearby are vegetable forms with long pointed leaves, like those of an aloe. Then, out of this luxuriant tropical growth, a tree trunk shoots upwards with broad, drooping leaves, like those of a palm, and from it hangs a large yellow fruit. Behind this tropical vegetation we see the broad surfaces of bare pyramidal forms—an oasis beside the desert highway? And on the left it seems as if the same configuration is trying to repeat itself in a distorted reflection—a mirage, Fata Morgana? That is what this picture reveals after prolonged scrutiny, and through the crystalline, abstract construction we recognize clearly a source of objective emotion. Now it becomes a landscape, and the deep blue of the sky transports us to the Mediterranean. The notes of pink and yellow lead us to suspect a desert in the vicinity, but the tropical vegetation suggests the sea. Thus it has brought to mind a landscape which we can even describe. This picture must have something to do with the African sea-board of the Mediterranean—proximity of a desert, Tripoli or Tunis. Tunis it is. Of course not the normal Tunisian landscape which one sees or paints, but an image of Tunis which imposed itself on Klee as a collective symbol and a pictorial equivalent. It is a memory of the country which he had visited with his friends, August Macke and Louis Moilliet, in the radiant spring of 1914.

Much has been made of this journey, and rightly, for it inspired many a treasure of German art. For example, the series of last great watercolours produced by August Macke, who died aged twenty-seven in September of the same year.

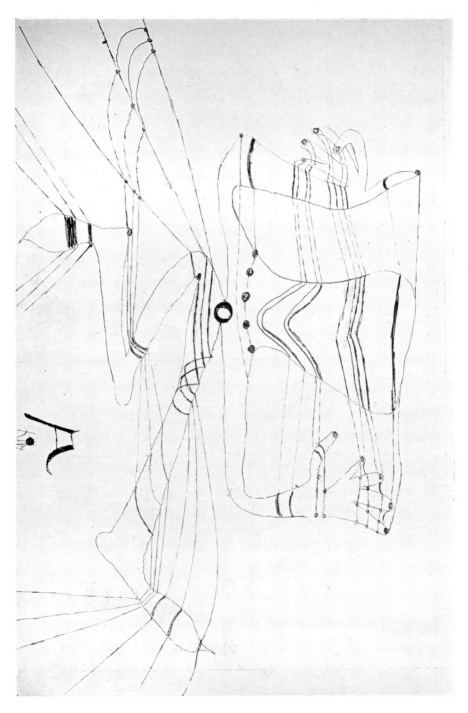

DANCE OF THE VEILS, 1920

Collection Ibach, Munich

AUTUMNAL PLACE, 1921
Private Collection, Munich

THE GIFT OF COLOUR

To Klee it brought the experience of colour, which he suddenly realized was an inherent element in Nature. The insight into the nature of colour, which he had been following from Cézanne to Delaunay, had at last become an everyday visual experience.

The extraordinary thing is that Klee's visit to Tunis lasted only twelve days. But for Klee, whose powers of visual appreciation were enormous, it sufficed. He had already planned the journey in the autumn of 1913, during conversations beside the Lake of Thun with Macke and Moilliet. Relying on the hospitality of a Swiss doctor in Tunis, they set out on 5th April 1914, travelling by way of Lyons, then across southern France, which had been sanctified by Cézanne and Van Gogh, to Marseilles. On 6th April they embarked, and on 7th April had reached the coast of Africa. Klee saw at once that it was the 'embodiment of a fairy-tale. The sun had a dark power. The land, light and colourful, seemed full of promise. Reality and dream simultaneously, to which was added, as a third element, the "self" I put into it'. Klee's immediate experience was that of losing his 'self' in nature. Art, Nature and the ego: these seemed now to form a whole. He began to work at once, no later than the following morning. The clear-cut architecture of the town seen in a bright light immediately suggested the formal synthesis of the pictorial structure. It all happened spontaneously. Out of a few broad, luminous patches of colour he produced a tectonic structure which needed only the addition of a few descriptive lines (such as the outlines of the domed roofs) to turn it into a complete, but independent, pictorial equivalent of nature. Everything was there, but as something personal and experienced: Cézanne's modulations, the *plans superposés* of the Cubists, Delaunay's arrangement of planes of colour. As something personal! The colour of the country had a wonderful appeal—the green, yellow and terracotta in front of the blue of the sea and the sky. 'The harmony has sunk in deep and will remain, even though I may not be painting on the spot.' How deep it sank in and how long it lasted is shown by our little picture of 1918.

By day Klee worked hard under the direct inspiration of the grandiose landscape. But on Easter Sunday, when a full moon rose in an indescribably beautiful evening sky, Klee had an idea for a picture. However he knew that it was premature for him to try and paint it. 'Still I do know rather more than before. I know the extent of the gap between Nature and what I am capable of. That depends on things within myself which I must develop during the next few years. I am not at all depressed about it. One must not be impatient if one wants so much. That evening is buried deep within me for ever. Many a blond northern moonrise, like a misty reflection, will gently remind me of it. It shall be my bride, my other self. It will be for me to provide the liberating impulse. But it is I who am the southern moon-rise.' Klee stored up within himself so many things which he knew would find their way out again. One such was the picture of which I am speaking.

Then there were expeditions! To St. Germain, to Hammamet; birds in ragged old bushes, dromedaries by wells, cemeteries beside the sea with animals—'that is good!' A blind minstrel led by a boy beating a tambourine was 'a rhythm forever'. And on 15th April, Klee was in Kairouan. 'Extract of the Arabian Nights with 99 per cent. reality content'. He painted a little, but his inner self was filled with amazement. 'I am giving up work for the present. It is all sinking so deeply and calmly into me. I can feel it and am becoming confident without doing anything. Colour has taken possession of me. That is the significance of this happy hour:

colour and I are one. I am a painter.' Klee was bubbling over
with his experience: it became too strong for him. The profusion of things he had seen—'most of them stored deep within
me, but I am so full that they may reappear at any moment'—

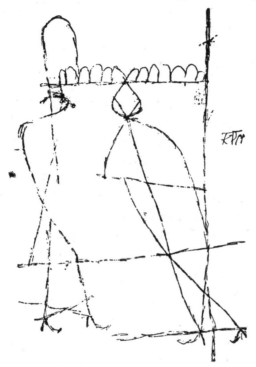

Kairouan (Sketch), 1914

induced in him a restless mood. He felt that he had to set to
work, so on 19th April he travelled home, alone. He hurried
from Naples towards the north without a stop lest the oriental
music within him should fade. Even the noise made by the
wheels of the train between Milan and Bern brought to mind
'the rhythm of the tambourine accompanying the song of the
blind man at Hammamet'.

67

There followed years of gestation, whilst the continent was ravaged by war. Coloured forms were Klee's chief concern and his pictorial structure became quite abstract. But beneath the abstract form lurked the genesis of the work. 'Creation exists as genesis beneath the visible surface of a work.' A theme from somewhere within himself identified itself with something seen, shapes began to form, growing as it were within a womb, and as they grew the male element which determines form took control, fashioned the structure according to the law of picture-making, and gave the growing forms an objective character, a designation. Form is the final result of both gestation and designation. 'From the means to the end. From what is actually living to something inactive. What counts in any work is its genesis as formal movement.' The artist in Klee had finally attained complete detachment and now inhabited a plane remote from the world: it was 'as though my only link with things was through memory'. Having attained to this remote and silent plane, he waited for pictures to well up from within himself.

> *A kind of stillness illumines the ground.*
> *From something vague*
> *a something shines,*
> *not from here,*
> *not from me,*
> *but of God.*[1]

Now if we turn back to our picture, we shall see it through

[1] *Eine Art von Stille leuchtet zum Grund*
Von ungefähr
scheint da ein Etwas,
nicht von hier,
nicht von mir,
sondern Gottes.

more knowing eyes. Something on the ground was illumined, one of those deeply submerged memories of a radiant African noon, as this vision of creation penetrated deep into Klee's being. Now, of its own accord, it begins to take shape: forms present themselves, growing this way and that, colours unite in harmony. Like a crystal its parts come together, the image struggles to perfect itself. But then the artist intervenes with his power of determining forms. He arranges the colour-structure in a series of planes, builds the forms tectonically into the picture and gives designations to the various objects —plant and sand, tree and sea. Studied and elaborated formal discoveries play their part: Delaunay's system of planes of colour, 'simultaneity', the 'dynamism' of the Futurists, and an exclamation mark borrowed from the Cubists, a small black thing which pushes the whole picture further away from us into an abstract distance, so that it seems as if we are looking at it through a pane of glass on which the exclamation mark is painted. Thus the picture is a crystallization of things ex-perienced, things which have grown, things which have been made and things which are known. Now if we look into this crystalline image, the 'something not from here' shines up at us 'from the ground', and we can see, if only our heart is open, what penetrated so deeply into Klee's soul and has emerged as form. We can experience it, because we have followed the genesis of the image, and that is what Klee meant by: 'creation exists as genesis beneath the visible surface of a work'. Really to understand Klee's pictures we must go back to their source.

The material on which this picture is painted gives us a small indication of the circumstances in which it was pro-duced, and this sends us back to biographical factors, to a consideration of Klee's situation. This picture is painted on a

fine silk-like material, aeroplane fabric, some bit of stuff that
he may have found lying about in an aeroplane hangar. For
Klee (who was by then aged 37) was called up for military
service in March 1916, and drafted as ground personnel in
the air force. Subsequently, he had the good fortune to be
transferred as a clerk on the administrative staff of a Bavarian
Flying Training School. There, as he sat at his desk, he was
able to work out pictorial images. Nothing else mattered to
him, for he had no interest in the war. 'I have had this war in
me for a long time, therefore it has no significance for my self
within. Now it is only in memory that I dwell in that shattered
world, when from time to time I look back on it. Thus I am
"abstract with memories".' Secretly, on a second precious
level of life, he cultivated his images. No matter how depres-
sing his life, he never lost his serenity or light-heartedness,
and putting on his magician's cloak would conjure up, with
the magic of coloured forms, those precious dreams, which
once were or once might be. On this second level of life there
was a fusion between things he knew about and things he had
experienced: Cubism and Futurism, the constructive and the
dynamic, the simultaneous and the static, the abstract and the
concrete. And the fusion produced a thoroughly individual
style tinged with a new breath of romanticism which never
declined into pathos.

To this period belong Klee's inscription-pictures (*Schriftbilder*), word-conjunctions to which Klee's artistic self heark-
ened and which he allowed to find their way through into
pictures. Lines of writing set in coloured squares and strips so
that the sound and meaning of the words is changed into
something visible through the play of letters of the alphabet
against a coloured background.[1]

[1] For example: *Einst dem Grau der Nacht enttaucht/Dann schwer und teuer und*

THE GIFT OF COLOUR

When Paul Klee was demobilized in 1919 he was a fully developed painter. He had mastered oil-painting, and proved it in a series of remarkable pictures: 'Composition with a Window', 'The Full Moon', 'The Rooster and the Grenadier'.

Let us analyse 'The Full Moon' and take stock of Klee's achievement. A series of crystalline forms grow towards the spectator out of a dark background—triangles and squares set in front of a plain surface. Considered formally, this structure breaks down into four flat spatial planes, lying parallel to the foreground plane. The similarity with the type of composition to be found in an early Cubist picture by Braque is obvious. Nevertheless, there is no point in insisting upon this comparison for it has no validity once one has become aware of the range of Klee's colour scheme, which runs from violet to orange. It reaches out, we might say, into a more romantic, more other-worldly sphere than do the noble, materialistic greys and ochres of an early Braque. And whereas Braque's forms are held together in a static harmony, Klee's have been given a peculiar zigzag movement. Starting from the base of the picture, Klee's small, pointed, rectangular forms seem to be climbing up to where the structure culminates in a sharp triangular point which is aimed at a tranquil, circular form. There seems to be a general upwards movement as if all the fragmentary forms were being magnetically attracted by the perfectly formed circle of gleaming light; and that small triangular point represents the area of greatest concentration, where the gap between the terrestrial and the cosmic is most

71

forcibly emphasized. The circle of light remains intangible. This moment of poetic expression is a purely formal experience and is made comprehensible to us through the upward-striving of the splinter-like forms, which are alternately dark and light. Their movement culminates in the triangular point which is opposed to something entirely different—a fully formed and perfectly rounded circle of light. 'The circle, the purest, the cosmic form of movement, only comes into being after the elimination of earthly restraints,' to quote a definition by Klee. Historically speaking, of course, it would be possible to show that this owed something to the dynamism of the Futurists. But, the forms indicating movement in Futurist pictures were formalized interpretations derived from observation of movement. Klee, on the other hand, only made use of such movement as he could produce with the pictorial means. Movement in Klee's pictures is an abstract expressive element which attempts, as the picture progresses, to acquire a poetic value by purely pictorial means. The pictorial image is an entirely abstract construction of classification and movement, which sways backwards and forwards until it finds its equilibrium. The balance is being constantly upset by conflicting values and has to be redressed by counterweights, but the work will have more character if the gap to be bridged between the opposing elements, which have to be reconciled, is a wide one. (The tranquil, hovering circle opposed to the staccato movement of the fragmentary pointed forms.) But the whole abstract structure moves towards an end: it aspires towards poetry, it longs for a name. And as classification proceeds 'the something from the ground' lights up again and reveals the name. The opposition between the terrestrial and the cosmic has been experienced in terms of form and it is this which prompts the choice of a title. The circle becomes a planet at rest in the cosmos; the pointed staccato forms belong to the realm of earthbound movement. Now with a very few signs, such as children or cartographers use, the whole image is rendered objectively legible. Three signs for trees—foliated, round-topped and coniferous—and already the earthly zone has been defined as mountainous country seen in the magic light of the moon. Then, on the left, a stocky well-rounded tree, such as might be found in a peasant's garden; and lastly a curtained window. That is all. But an abstract construction has been made to correspond to something material. And there is something more: the 'simultaneous' elements coincide with the static. Here—and once again the historian may be reminded of the 'simultaneity' of Delaunay and the Futurists—Klee has succeeded in packing signs of very different kinds into a single picture, though in reality they could not all be visible simultaneously: house, orchard, mountains, forests, terrestrial forces and a planet. But the 'simultaneous' elements have been given the suggestive value of hieroglyphs by some slight indications which explain the forms to us. The static domain of form is not affected; it is simply over-printed with unobtrusive 'simultaneous' signs to make it easier for our imagination to follow the right paths.

This analysis has enabled us to explain the mysterious connection between all the various ideas which Klee (who was now forty) had picked up as he went along. For he had made a synthesis of the constructive and the dynamic, the abstract and the concrete, the simultaneous and the static. And through hard work, helped by ideas borrowed from the Cubists, the Futurists, and Delaunay, he had at last achieved a style of his own which enabled him to draw on realms which had hitherto proved beyond the artist's reach. By psychic improvisation he was now able to communicate experiences which had taken shape within the realm of the soul.

What is the purpose of this picture? One could go on explaining it in poetic terms until ultimately the whole of Jean Paul's[1] world would have been discovered in this one picture. Did Klee intend this or something else? 'Abstract with memories', he is searching within himself, has become his own spectator, and is seeking to reveal in poetic-pictorial terms 'a something from the ground', an experience that shines through from afar. This takes shape within himself, and then becomes a part of his conscious personality. Have we forgotten what he wrote about the moonrise in Tunisia? 'Many a blond northern moonrise, like a misty reflection, will gently remind me of it. It shall be my bride, my other self. It will be for me to provide the liberating impulse.' The purpose of this picture is therefore to reveal to us visually an amalgam of Nature and Man. Pictorially, nature and the spiritual experience must be made to cohere with the unity of a crystalline formation, so that the image is both a pure communication from the world of human expression and a work in which creation lives as genesis below the surface. Klee could then feel that he had bridged 'the gap between Nature and his own incapacity as an artist', and that the whole world complex embracing man and nature could become the subject of painting.

[1] A German romantic writer (1763–1825) whom Klee particularly admired. (Translator's note.)

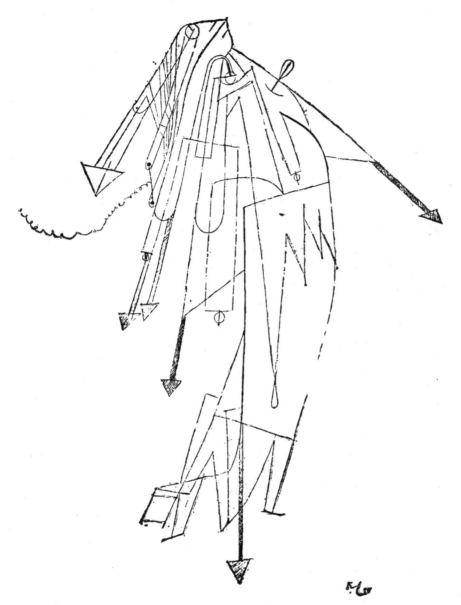

Going to the Dance of the Fly-By-Nights, 1922

75

Chapter V

THE MASTER AT THE BAUHAUS

This was a great idea, and in the stimulating atmosphere of post-war Germany it was recognized as such by a small group of men. This meant the end of misunderstanding, the end also of being labelled a playful Expressionist, a man possessed by excessive intuition who covered his canvases with emotional visions of the objective world.

That style of painting, which appeared so significant at the time, was incapable of development, so Klee turned his back on it and cultivated instead a form of art based on a keen intelligence and an insight into the crystalline growth of artistic images.

In 1920, Klee's fame was surprisingly well established. Hans Goltz organized the first large-scale exhibition of his work, an exhibition of over three hundred works, including drawings, prints, paintings and sculpture. These last were grotesque, small, abstract figurines, which Klee had made in his Munich days when he was trying to find out more about spatial relationships and the transformation of natural shapes into their formal equivalents. No less than three small monographs on Klee appeared, by Hausenstein, Wedderkop and Zahn. Kurt Wolff published Voltaire's *Candide* with illustrations by Klee, and Georg Müller asked Klee to illustrate C. Corrinth's abstruse but ecstatic book *Potsdamer Platz oder die Nächte des neuen Messias*.[1] These new illustrative drawings display Klee's perfect control of line, with which he is able vividly to suggest a subject even when he seems most determined to avoid pictorial representation. 'Higher, then dwindling', is the title of the last drawing of the series. On the right of this drawing, rising out of turmoil at the base which echoes with the sound of voices, we see a barren garden of shapeless, sexual passions. On the left, the apotheosis of the apostle of free love is given a purer and less worldly setting. The whole content is however expressed simply through the suggestive power of pure line, which responds gracefully to the subtlest demands of psychic improvization but at the same time builds up a solid and well-ordered structure of independent value. This formative, tectonic tendency distinguishes Klee's art sharply from Expressionism and situates it in a more definitely constructive line of development, which originated in architecture, where it led to functionalism, and then spread to painting, where it took the form of Constructivism and Suprematism, and reached its purest expression in the work of Piet Mondrian. The internal consistency which stamped the whole silently growing life of Klee, brought him now into an environment where such ideas were flourishing while being directed towards a common purpose.

In 1920, the architect Walter Gropius approached Klee and offered him a post as teacher in the newly-founded Bauhaus at Weimar. Modern art flourished in Weimar. In 1902, van de Velde had been summoned by the Grand Duke of Saxe-Weimar to organize a school of Arts and Crafts there, and it was on the advice of van de Velde that the last Grand Duke

---

[1] Published by Müller of Munich in 1920 with ten drawings by Klee reproduced in photolithography. (Translator's note.)

had summoned Gropius to succeed him. Gropius, who took up the post in 1919, found himself at the head of a new institute which had been created by amalgamating the Academy of Fine Arts with the School of Arts and Crafts and adding an architectural department. Gropius had the advantage of being able to start all over again. He persuaded the painter Lyonel Feininger to join the faculty of masters, as well as the sculptor Gerhardt Marcks. Johannes Itten, a painter and pedagogue who had been trained at Adolf Hoelzel's school, also joined and handed on his master's theories of pictorial harmony. All these men had a common obsession with form and they subsequently extended invitations to join them to the architect Adolf Meyer in 1919, to the painter Georg Muche in 1920, to Paul Klee in January 1921 and to Oskar Schlemmer and Lothar Schreyer in April. Kandinsky joined them in 1922 and Moholy-Nagy in 1923.

The Bauhaus made no distinction between artists and craftsmen. The artist was regarded as 'an exalted' craftsman, but good workmanship was considered an essential attribute of every artist. Gropius set forth his aims in a proclamation in April 1919: 'Together let us conceive and create the new building of the future, which will embrace everything, architecture, sculpture and painting, in one unity and will rise one day toward heaven from the hands of a million workers like the crystalline symbol of a new and coming faith.' So the teachers were called 'Masters of Form' and the students were called apprentices, and each had to have a specimen of his journeyman work accepted by the guild of craftsmen. Every student had to attend a preliminary course, devised by Itten, in which he was allowed to work freely in different materials. This enabled the masters to decide on the particular nature of his gifts and to advise on the best way of using them. The

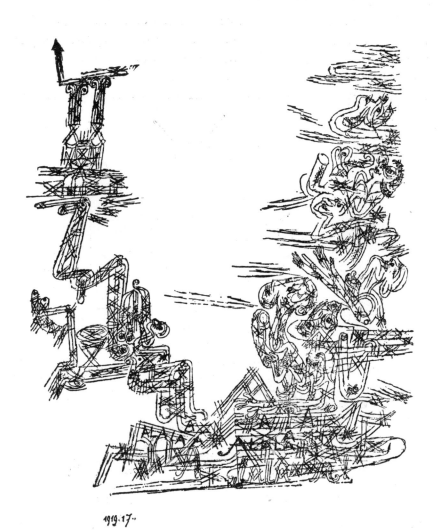

1919·17··

*Higher, **then** dwindling, Illustration for C. Corrinth's
'Potsdamer Platz', 1919*

79

Bauhaus remained in Weimar from 1919 to 1924, and during these years functionalism as an idea continued to gain ground; then in 1925, as a result of political attacks, it moved to Dessau In 1928 Gropius resigned and was succeeded by the Swiss architect, Hannes Meyer, under whom serious internal crises

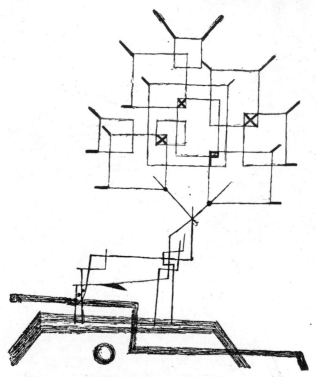

The Stag, 1918, *Klee Gesellschaft, Bern*

developed, for Meyer refused to have anything to do with painting. And so, seeing the break-up of the close community of the Bauhaus at hand, and fearing the increasingly violent political attacks that were being made on it, Klee in 1930 accepted the offer of a post at the Academy of Fine Arts in

FISHES, 1921
Private Collection, Hamburg

EXERCITIUM IN BLUE AND ORANGE, 1924
Private Collection, Munich

Düsseldorf. But the ten years he spent in the working community of the Bauhaus were among the most decisive of his life, for they provided him with the stimulus of human and artistic contacts. He was able constantly to exchange ideas with such important artists as Kandinsky, Schlemmer and Feininger, was united with them in a great common purpose, and had the responsibility of communicating this purpose to a younger generation.

Like Kandinsky, Klee had a painting class. His first responsibility as a Master of Form, was to take charge of glass-painting, then of weaving, and in Klee's work of this date one is often conscious of his preoccupation with the handling of colour and form in these two techniques. He attached great importance to theoretical teaching. Klee gave regular and methodical lectures on the fundamentals of painting: the pictorial means and the genesis of forms and colours. He referred to this vast subject as 'orientation on the formal plane', and he set problems arising out of this theoretical study which his students had to work out on their own. Once a week the results were discussed in Klee's studio, but in the course of criticizing individual solutions Klee would avail himself of the opportunity to discourse at length on the fundamental genetic principles of painting.

Klee worked closely together with Kandinsky both as teacher and as artist. Indeed at times the resemblance between their work is so close that an untrained eye might well confuse it. When Kandinsky arrived in Weimar in 1922, his painting was essentially constructive in aim; he used precise geometrical forms and primary colours to build up an abstract basis for his picture. But Klee too, who had cautiously allowed things to develop slowly, had already turned towards constructivism. A sheet like 'Autumnal Place' of 1921 (the year

F

in which Klee went to the Bauhaus) is noticeably firmer and more crystalline than the last picture which I described, 'Full Moon' of 1919. The picture is traversed by a system of scaffolding which binds the forms and spatial planes rigidly together. As teachers, Klee and Kandinsky followed very much the same principles. Kandinsky was convinced that he could formulate an exact theory of pictorial harmony, and he devoted himself to studying each pictorial element, separately and scientifically, as if it were under a microscope. In the course of a lecture he would group a few objects together and abstract from them a logical structure of lines and patches of colour. He then analysed this structure in terms of the pictorial means—point, line, surface, space and so on. That seemed very like Klee's procedure, yet there was a great difference between the two men and they complemented each other wonderfully. Klee regarded the pictorial means as a productive force. Right from the start he treated them as a highly independent force which had to be allowed to grow genetically, for during this process of growth he was continually led on to say something new. Kandinsky stuck rigidly to his means and proceeded to apply them logically, calmly and constructively. He cast around for a structure, pinned it down and built up his picture from that basis. Klee proceeded from a germ of form within himself which he allowed to develop rhythmically. Direct construction seemed to him like a short cut, and he distrusted such procedures. Kandinsky took hold of the world but remained outside it. Klee sank himself in the world. Klee did not decide on a construction in advance; he looked for an underlying order which would yield up a construction after he had found it. And this order certainly involved a more complicated but also a richer world. As a method of teaching, Kandinsky's system was more generally practicable. Klee on the other hand addressed himself to solitary meditative spirits. Thus, by their very differences, which were inherent in their characters, they complemented each other, and this proved of great value to teachers and students alike.

When Klee went to teach at the Bauhaus, he felt that it was his first duty 'to be absolutely clear about what he—unconsciously for the most part—did'. This process of clarification was immensely productive and helped Klee to reach new and more definite conclusions. He liked to tell his pupils that it was really himself who should be paying, because he was learning so much from his own teaching. So now I shall attempt to describe Klee's system of teaching, because there at least we can be sure of making contact with his own ways of pictorial thinking. And after we have followed him through the domain of the pictorial means and considered his attitude to natural objects we shall inevitably reach the realm in which his pictures arc born. Thus we shall find what is at the heart of a picture by Klee.

One of the foundations of Klee's teaching was that no artist, and much less a student, should rely on ready-made forms, because ready-made forms are the outcome of the progressive investigations of others or of oneself. And one cannot begin at the end. The whole point in art is to set about it in the right way. Early in life, in 1902, Klee had written in his diary: 'It is most necessary to have to begin with something small.' And in 1923, while teaching at the Bauhaus, he said to his pupils: 'You will never achieve anything unless you work up towards it. You can't break in halfway through the process, and least of all can you start with a result. You must start at the beginning. Then you will avoid all trace of artificiality, and the creative process will function without interruption.' By this he meant that the 'origin' had to be within oneself, and that one should begin with tiny but real acts.

So it fitted entirely with Klee's ideas that the preliminary course at the Bauhaus should consist of materials which had nothing to do with 'Art'. Piles of old cloth, paper, pasteboard, old wall-paper, steel filings, tinfoil, glass, spun glass, cellophane etc.—were put at the disposal of the students in the workshop. These materials then had to be closely studied, their nature and special properties described and tested and suggestions made for their use—it might be a technical or a theoretical use, but not necessarily artistic. This exercise was a way of distinguishing between the aptitude of the various students.

The would-be artist had first of all to forget about everything he had done before, he had to sublimate his personality and, through an act of self-negation, become passively receptive towards the material in which he was working. In other words he had to find a reason for working which had nothing to do with wanting to make 'art' and had to be content to allow the substance of the material to inspire him to creation. He had to look, then look again. He had to analyse and compare—for example, the fundamental differences between paper and steel, or between tar-paper and glass—he had to demonstrate what he had discovered and then he had to prove it not only to himself but to others by constructions made of several materials.

The imagination began to work on a serious plane through contact with some raw material. The student was free to do anything he liked provided he could justify it in terms of the material; his will to create was brought into play by its powers of suggestion. The material seemed to demand that something should be done or made with it, secure in the feeling that it had been thoroughly understood and that it had provoked a sharpening of the senses. But the effect of any such sharpening is to produce amazement. Therefore the first lesson to learn was to be prepared for amazement. This Klee left to be learnt from materials alone.

Some explanation for this had to be found. The combination of amazement and search for an explanation then stimulated the first really pictorial act, because objects have to be put together, arranged, and experimentally set in motion. At that point the game ceases and becomes a form of pictorial research—'*méthode de la recherche*'. For while attempting to compose with wood and glass, or sand and steel, unexpected and surprising things often happen. Work leading to discovery and thus becoming a new source of surprise! Naturally, therefore, words such as 'interesting', 'cunning' or 'sensational' acquired an ethical significance when applied to the thing created, because they appeared to be surprising epithets to apply to the results of a trial-and-error procedure. Having arrived at a combination by trial-and-error, and granted the polyphony of the materials, anything surprising seemed to have happened naturally and therefore appeared as a new-found beauty. This new, and hitherto unknown, beauty consists not only of sensuous visual values (colour, light and line) or tactile values (structure), but also of respect for their nature. This peculiar blend of analysis, of combination and of magic, can only be produced by working with means which originally had no artistic application. The process of combining objects gives the spiritual direction and leads to that polyphony, which, on the formal plane, we call composition, and on the spiritual plane, an expressive formula. Taken as a whole, the result is a tiny but real image which exists purely and logically on three planes. If the student starts from the existential properties of objects, the work of classifying and combining them will lead him to a spiritual plane, and the indeterminate spiritual value which is inherent in the material will find visible expression in some construction. Something new comes into being, a product of his soul responding to the challenge of everyday things. In the language of psychology, this is called an expressive formulation of surprise.

This certainly gave students a most unexpected glimpse into the domain of art. But it was only a glimpse, because they could only experiment with materials and objects in their immediate surroundings, and were confined to actually existing things. Nevertheless, there was a little mystery about the resulting construction, something unexpected, and this unexpected element appeared at the end of a logical development, and was therefore ultimately justifiable.

The whole point of the exercise was that a seemingly purposeless pastime should provide an experience which could subsequently be turned to artistic ends. After that a new pictorial means was discovered: the formless material was turned into a pictorial means adapted to the purpose of representation. Material and object became the formal roots out of which the image grew. Even in the most elementary painting class Klee taught his students: 'Not form, but forming, not form as a final appearance, but form in the process of becoming, as genesis.' The budding artist was taught the pictorial means in a laboratory. His whole activity was directed towards changing things, towards transforming insignificant things into pictorial means. But that implies enlarging the arsenal of artistic creation, finding a soul in insignificant things bringing inanimate things to life. The first small but real act in Klee's sense was the freeing of objects and materials from an inanimate state, thereby enabling them to communicate something.

The method was typical of the period. In fact between 1914 and 1920, that is to say before Klee went to the Bauhaus as a teacher, the possibilities of such a procedure had been exploited by the movement known as Dadaism. In 1916, in the hectic émigré atmosphere of Zurich, Tristan Tzara, in company with Arp, Apollinaire and others, had published revolutionary Dada proclamations. The movement had spread to New York with Duchamp, Picabia and Man Ray, to Paris with Aragon, Eluard, Ribemont-Dessaignes and Breton, to Cologne with Max Ernst, Arp and Baargeld, to Hanover with Schwitters, to Berlin with Grosz, Schlichter and Mehring. By 1920, the Dada movement was at its height and wild Dadaist exhibitions were held in Berlin, Cologne and Paris. This movement gave the impression of being anything but serious; it exalted the mad, the satirical, the accidental, the perverted, the unfettered, the convulsive. It was directed against 'art'. But as it followed its course it came up against objects. Marcel Duchamp invented the 'ready-made', that is to say some everyday object—a plate-rack or an urinal—which he exhibited unadorned, just as he had found it, thereby creating the impression that it was something which might have been found by magic. The thing thus appeared surprising and was indeed intended to cause surprise. Kurt Schwitters cultivated astonishing confrontations more actively by collecting rubbish of all sorts—pickings from dust-bins, bus-tickets, waste-paper—out of which he constructed new, surprising and disquieting objects. The idea had originated with the pasted papers of Braque and Picasso in 1912. When put to positive creative use, Dada's discoveries were not altogether insignificant. They consisted in a systematic search for latent possibilities in objects and materials which could serve the purpose of pictorial representation. Objects were accepted in their literal sense, they were forced to reveal their secrets and were deliberately brought into juxtaposition with other objects in order to provoke a communication. Klee observed the processes used by Dada attentively and recommended them to his pupils. For secretly he knew that the height of absurdity is reached when man feels that the objects around him are nameless, and that only by approaching absurdity will he be able to find a name, a description and a sign for them.

The questioning of objects has been one of the strongest impulses to artistic creation during this century. It began with Cézanne, in whose work objects attained an independent and challenging existence. Now it is not purely a question of love; hate too plays its part. Rilke felt this when he remarked in 1907 that Cézanne had proved the need 'for transcending even love. It is indeed natural for one to love every one of these objects, if one has made it: but if one shows that, then one makes it less well, because one forms an opinion of it, instead of stating it. One paints "I love this", instead of stating "here it is".' The aggressive presence of objects made them disquieting allies in the modern attempt to dominate the world. They were everywhere, forcing themselves upon man, motionless, dumb. It was their silence and immobility which made them appear sinister and disquieting, and this gave rise to the feeling that they were permanently challenging. Kafka has described this feeling. Modern literature consistently avoids dramatic events or a plot; it is to a great extent concerned with man's attempts to come to terms with the things around him. Painting too has become more concerned with objects as still-life has become the chief subject. And *Angst*, even hatred, has appeared there too. Thus we see the Cubists, in about 1909, analysing and dissecting objects in order to make an ordered pictorial arrangement out of the fragments. The Italian '*Pittura Metafisica*' of 1917 too was an attempt to exploit the mystery of the unexpected, the lyrical properties of trivial things, the enchanted pathos of objects which had been silently forgotten. Thus a tailor's dummy stands motionless between some forgotten biscuits and a metal fish in a room which fills with magic as a result of this juxtaposition. Then Dada fastened on objects, and having overpowered them threw them to the Surrealists. The latter resorted to an even stranger process: they placed things in unusual surroundings (a milk-can on a rocky island, furniture on a sea-shore) and depicted the sensations that developed as a result of these new relationships. The effect of this on the objects was so dramatic as to provoke fear. Silence and immobility are the cause of this fear; also a little hatred on our part.

But there is also another way, that of stopping and listening for a response in ourselves. That means becoming intimate with objects, reaching a stage where their image is not blurred by passion, where we can wait attentively and silently until the essence of their being is revealed. This new knowledge comes because objects communicate as an answering reflex within ourselves, and only the man who understands the communication, who reflects objects, will receive it. Hence Marcel Proust, certain no doubt of an affirmative answer, hesitantly asked whether 'the immobility of the objects around us is not simply imposed on them by our certainty that they are one particular thing and not something else, that is to say by the fixed nature of our ideas about them'. An attempt therefore had to be made to broaden man's outlook and eliminate anxiety. 'Even evil shall no longer be a triumphant or shaming enemy but a force co-operating towards a Whole,' said Klee. The artist's ego and the object's self must be comprehensible as a unity within the compact structure of the universe. They must have common roots in the earth below and must also meet in the cosmos above. The unity of this structure is composed of ego and object, cosmic and earthly elements. Each separate element of this structure is only a fragment. At that point Klee proudly proclaimed: 'Formerly the painter depicted objects which were to be seen on earth, things he liked or would have liked to see. Now the real nature of visible things is revealed, and so the belief becomes reality that, in terms of the universe, what is visible is but a fragment of the whole, there being many more latent realities. Things appear both magnified and multiplied, and often in contradiction with the rational experience of yesterday. So an attempt must be made to eliminate the accidental.' Such was the new reality which was pursued everywhere. So there is nothing surprising about the fact that while Klee was dumping an assortment of materials on the work-tables of his students at the Bauhaus, another painter in another corner of Europe—Carlo Carrà—was writing: 'Everyday objects reveal those forms of simplicity, which enable us to recognize a higher and more fundamental state of being; in this resides the whole mysterious grandeur of art.'

Now for perspective. With the aid of the technical premises of speed, civilizing man has continued during this century to reduce spatial distances. But he has failed to get 'near' to objects, and so far as objects are concerned has only elevated 'near' and 'far' relationships into 'distanceless' ones. Meanwhile, however, aesthetic man, with the aid of the premises of art, has crept close to the secrets of objects and has begun to listen-in to their communications. These are abstract and spiritual communications for which he is seeking an appropriate means of expression with the purpose, as Klee said, of 'ultimately creating a formal cosmos, which shall so completely resemble the great work of the creator that breath alone will suffice to turn an expression of religious sentiments into reality'. The reflected image of the world!

Drawing with the Pause-Sign, 1918

Chapter VI

THE PEDAGOGICAL SKETCHBOOK

S peaking pictorially, the problem is to find a language
to express our responses (that is to say the responses
involving the whole four-fold structure. In painting
the words of this language are formed by the use that
we make of the pictorial means. And experience taught Klee
that the pictorial elements constitute an instrument which
has been given to man to create an imaginary world of experience, parallel to, yet reflecting, the world of reality (that
is to say transcending the four-fold formal unity) and therefore endowed with human significance. Further, he believed
that if the artist's use of these elements is pure, he will discover nothing that is arbitrary, that is to say nothing which
does not already exist in the world taken as a whole. Thus, in
Klee's view, any play of rhythms set up by or made percep-
tible through the pictorial means, inevitably corresponds to
some rhythm in nature, whether it be the rhythm of a man's
walk, a man's breathing, or a man's heart beating, or whether
on the other hand it be the cosmic rhythms of day and night,
of year succeeding year, or of the moon in relation to the earth.
As Klee stood at the large blackboard of his class-room, drawing often with both hands, and spoke with urgency in his soft
voice of the necessity of 'giving directions on the formal plane'

and of 'cultivating the purest use of the pictorial means', the most simple element suddenly became an active personality and began to communicate its message. In a small volume— *Pedagogical Sketchbook (Pädagogisches Skizzenbuch)*[1]—written by Klee in 1924 and published by the Bauhaus in 1925, are preserved some samples of his teaching method. They are not entirely comprehensible on their own. So here I shall try to indicate the general trend of his views on how to master the formal means, supplementing this with references to pictures, with records of conversations with students and with quotations from his own writings.

Klee began with the simplest example, with something that came of its own accord: a dot. Now it is worth noting that Kandinsky wrote thirty pages of closely reasoned text on the pictorial significance of the dot and still felt obliged to excuse himself for the brevity of his explanation. Next, the dot was set in motion. This produced line, a line 'which moves freely; a walk for a walk's sake'. The agent: a shifting dot.

In this first little pictorial operation Klee already recognized that movement was inherent in the dynamic character of the pictorial means, and thus introduced the time-element. This tiny act inspired Klee's first key-sentences: 'Movement is the basis of all becoming. When a dot becomes movement and line, time is involved—a work of art is built up, piece by piece, just like a house. Scene of the action: time. Character: movement. Even in the universe movement is certain. The stand-

---

[1] An English translation by Sibyl Moholy-Nagy has recently been published: *The Pedagogical Sketchbook* (London and New York, 1953). (See p. 208.)

still on earth is a fortuitous harnessing of matter. To regard this standstill as a primary fact is to deceive oneself. The genesis of writing provides a very good parallel for movement. A work of art is also first and foremost a genesis; it is never experienced ready made. Paths are cut through a work of art for the venturesome eye of the spectator as though it might be an animal grazing. The eye follows the paths prepared for it through the work of art. The pictorial work originated in movement, is in itself recorded movement and is received as movement.'

An active line can be enhanced with complementary forms:

and in this way a little polyphony is created around a firm melody. Or the line circumscribes itself:

turns itself into movement, becomes baroque and tends towards richness, but also to confusion. It acquires polarity: richness and confusion. This polarity even leaves room for the expression of psychic elements. Or two secondary lines play around a central line, which is itself invisible.

Then the active line becomes imaginary; it exists as an 'idea' underlying the secondary lines, is the effective power, yet is not itself present.

With these first acts already the path towards the realm of

poetic understanding was sketched out through the use of pictorial means, and a small pictorial element has been allowed to communicate big things. Let us use one of Klee's own fables: 'Suppose we develop this idea, suppose we plot a topographical map and make a little journey into the land of fuller understanding. Let the first act of motion be set beyond the dead point (line). After a short time, pause to draw breath (broken line or, if repeated, rhythmically interrupted line). A backward look to see how far we have already gone (countermovement). Weighing up intellectually the distance between here and there (bundle of lines). A river seeks to hinder us, we take advantage of a boat (wavy movement). Higher up there is said to have been a bridge (series of arches). On the other side of the river we meet someone with the same ideas, who also wants to go where he can find greater understanding. At first we are united in joy (convergence), then gradually differences intrude (two lines moving independently). A certain excitement on both sides (expression, dynamism, and psyche of line). We cross an untended field (surface traversed by lines)—then a dense forest. He loses himself, looks around and once even goes through the classic movement of a dog running. I too am no longer quite cool: another river is lost in fog. But this is soon left behind. Basket weavers are going home with their cart (the wheel); beside one of them is a child with the funniest curls (spiral movement). Later it becomes muggy and nocturnal. A flash of lightning on the horizon (zigzag line). Over our heads the stars are still apparent (a series of dots). Soon our first sleeping quarters are reached. Before we fall asleep, much will recur in our memory, for even such a brief journey is full of impressions.'

Now let us permit this narrow field of the pictorial element to develop a little on its own, in order to advance, by more elaborate combinations, towards an image. The active line, given time, can progress from one point to the next; in this way it can reunite with itself and make a figure—rectangle, triangle, circle.

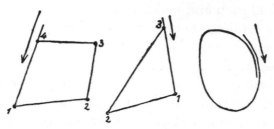

In the process of becoming, these figures have a linear character; once completed, the linear character is irrevocably replaced by the planes created. The line loses its active quality and assumes the character of an intermediary. As the pure contour of a form or plane it becomes absolutely passive. These qualities—active, medial, passive—are the expressive qualities of each element; within the whole complex organization of the pictorial means, they are the threads linking the individual elements together.

Thus through the medium of line we have entered the realm of planes, yet we still remain within the realm of measurement. For points, lines and planes are measurable; they are the formal means of measurement.

The element which unifies the surface and produces movement is structure. This appears as structural rhythm, and may take the form of a primitive arrangement in layers or of a highly complex series of accents. Its distinguishing mark is the repetition of some unit. Parts can be added or taken away without altering the rhythmic character, which depends on repetition. Key-sentence: structural character is dividual.

Now if I deprive the structure of its dividual character, I

am faced with an articulated relationship between individual elements. This can never be reduced to 1, so I have entered the realm of proportion: for example the equation a: b = b: (a +b) = The Golden Section. The realm of structure and of proportion is the home of rhythm; it is a domain of order and lucidity and is subject to the rule of law. There an interminable repetition

is given a visually comprehensible form such as this:

or this:

But the laws determining this rhythm are natural laws. And this opens up a perspective: 'The great thing in life is the hierarchy among objects and the relationship between individual components; by this means the whole is elevated to a symbolic standard of measurement.' Rhythmic construction too originates in small beginnings. Let us proceed by little steps. We draw a composite unit:

or

and increase it in one case by accumulation:

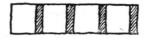

in another by alternation:

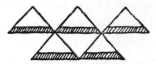

Now we enrich both with reflections of themselves:

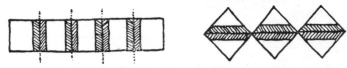

Now by turning the basic element, for example:

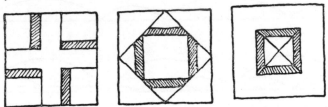

Now let us take another element, for example:

It then looks like this:

accumulated	reflected	in different positions

Even such minor manipulations of a tiny element produce a host of possible rhythmic relationships, and after a schematic demonstration of this kind, Klee would send his students home to work out on their own at least fifty other possible combinations, starting from this basic scheme. He would also warn them: 'Don't think of form but of forming. Stick to the main road, to preserving unbroken the continuity with your original idea.' Then, at the end, in order to make them forget about the petty detail of the pictorial element and think about higher things, Klee would ask for a single image expressing the unity behind the variety of designs which they had been working on, something which could serve as a symbolic centre-piece.

Then he would draw:

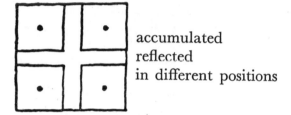

accumulated
reflected
in different positions

Such was Klee's system: to get something in motion and then let it come to rest. On the way, in his 'progress in the direction of critical rejection', he found a higher state of repose and order. The highest state of all was the work of art, which was also the outcome of a logical growth.

Now let us look inquiringly at nature, for which the pictorial means is an explanatory simile. We have already encountered dividual structure and we meet with it again in the material structures of Nature, in the grouping of the smallest recognizable components of matter. In the human body; for instance, in the structure of bones, tendons, and muscles. But in order to transform these into an organism capable of movement, we are once again involved in a relationship between individual parts. This hierarchy of movement is expressed in the same three concepts as before: active, medial, passive. The

99

function of bone in relation to muscle is passive, but muscle obeys the brain. So the following hierarchy is created: brain (active), muscle (medial), bone (passive). Klee then took this recurring triad and set his students the problem of explaining the relationship between these forces pictorially. He found his own solution in an image of a water-wheel and a hammer, thus:

Water Current=active; system of wheels=medial; the hammer=passive. Having become aware of this the emboldened spirit can now pass from one domain to another. It sees that the trichotomy is a property of line, finds it again as part of the transition from a structural to an articulated surface rhythm, recognizes it in the organic movements of nature (for example, in the growth of plants, which proceeds from the active realm of seed, roots and earth, through the medial realm of branches and leaves, to the passive act of blossoming), and discovers it once more in the circulation of the blood (the active heart, the passive blood, the medial lungs). Having once penetrated into a world so full of perspectives, the concepts 'active' and 'passive' take on meaning in other domains of expression—male and female, for instance, or, in terms of pictorial art, building up and hacking out, or, in terms of human activity, productive and receptive. And the work of art is all of this. 'The work as human activity (genesis) is productive as well as receptive.' Klee set great store by opening up such perspectives. For he wanted everything to be tense and in flux while yet remaining part of a whole; he wanted everything derived from doing, seeing or recognizing to appear to be held fast within the unity of the four-fold structure, which comprises the ego and the object, cosmic and earthly elements.

The field of operations dealt with so far can be considerably extended by the importation of a third dimension, the dimension of space. This is the realm of perspective. It is of course determined by things which are measurable, yet it is always related to the standpoint and field of vision of the subject—therefore it is mobile. A move to the left or right entails an alteration in the vertical structure of the perspective. The horizontal signifies the height (which is also very variable) of the subject (eye level). This human connection is pictorially important. A spatial construction can be logically right and yet appear false—hence, psychological mobility. For instance: 'In the interests of its own equilibrium an animal wants to see certain verticals in reality projected as verticals. The vertical signifies the direct way, the animal's upright bearing or stance; the horizontal signifies its height, its horizon. Both are thoroughly real static facts.'

The relationship between the perpendicular and the horizontal involves that vital domain of pictorial experiment—balance. There the key-image is that of a pair of scales. The first requirement of the human spirit is that a balance should exist between the different elements: at its simplest this is achieved by symmetry, on a higher level by asymmetry. Each time a pictorial element is moved the balance is disturbed, and this calls for a readjustment on a different level. 'The process of weighing starts from a lack of balance and finishes when balance has been found.' In a higher world of form, balance is obtained by a succession of incipient productive movements which are corrected by counter-movements; this complex fluctuation of arrested attempts at movement, which is reflected in the scales, provides the artist with dramatic possibilities of expression, but at the same time it makes him look critically at the world in general. He looks at nature: there he notices how the first movements a man makes in walking disturb his balance, how this is redressed by counter-movements, and how this leads to a complicated rhythm of marching, walking, dancing—which are expressive of how the body feels. Or in the field of statics: as the artist goes on building his complex structure, he will feel each loss of balance and its inevitable compensation as a motive impulse until 'he places the final stone and thus establishes a definitive equilibrium'.

But we are still in the earthly realm, and our symbols of this static realm are the plummet and the pair of scales, because they are the best pointers towards the earth's centre. 'But there are regions with other laws and new symbols, where movement is freer and positions more variable.' There the balance of our firm construction (perpendicular-horizontal) can be transformed into a loosely articulated relationship. For example, in air: altering the rigid static construction of an arch into the free line of a ballistic curve. Or elevated to the cosmic realm: the trajectory of a meteor, diverted from its course by the presence of a star.

As we can see from our two examples this new 'free equilibrium' comes about through the movement of forms. The symbolic form of the pair of scales turns into the symbolic form of the top. If we deprive the scales of its links with the ground, it will lose its balance and fall; but if we set it turning, it will be held upright and in balance by its own gyration. In moving forms therefore the top replaces the scales. The plummet becomes a pendulum (equilibrium being maintained by movement and counter-movement), whose form in motion can be expanded by moving the point at which it is held. And if the pendulum is freed from gravity and swings round, it produces a circle, or, by altering the length of its radius, a spiral. But now let Klee tell us about the higher symbols of forms in motion, then we may visualize how, after long and exact study, his uncompromising use of the pictorial elements led to pure poetic creation.

'The Circle: This purest mobile form, the cosmic one, is only created by the suspension of gravity, through the elimination of earthly ties.'

'The Spiral: Changing length of the radius, combined with peripheral movement, transforms the circle into the spiral. Lengthening of the radius creates a vibrant spiral. Shortening of the radius narrows the curve more and more, till the lovely spectacle suddenly dies in a static central point. Motion is no longer infinite there, so that the question of direction once again becomes important, and the choice of direction determines whether it will be a gradual liberation from the centre in increasingly free motions, or an increasing dependence on an ultimately destructive centre. This is a matter of life or death, and the decision rests with a little arrow.'

'The Arrow: The father of the arrow is the question, How do I extend my reach to that point over there? Over this river? this lake? that mountain? Man's ideological capacity to traverse at will both terrestrial and heavenly regions is in contrast to his physical impotence; this is the origin of all human tragedy. It is this contrast between power and powerlessness which produces the dichotomy of human existence. Half-winged, half-prisoner, such is man.

Thought as the intermediary between the earth and the universe. The longer the journey, the more heartrending the tragedy. To be impelled towards motion and not to achieve it.

Action bears this out. How does the arrow overcome the hindering friction? Never quite to reach the point where movement is endless! Discovery that where there is a beginning, there is never an infinity. Consolation: a bit further than usual —than possible?'

Each pictorial element was for Klee a silent living thing, a crystal for contemplation, enclosing within itself a glowing image of its own world.

Now let us look back. What have we traversed? We notice that, despite all our efforts, we are still on one level, that of measurement. We have developed it from a dot to a line to a plane. We have classified it by means of structure, proportion and rhythm, and extended it into a third dimension through perspective. Then we made it mobile by intervening (loss of balance and compensation) and demanding a changing and living equilibrium. And this led us to recognize that yet more subtle states of equilibrium result through the transformation of something static into something dynamic, through forms in motion. We believe similarly in the fourth dimension, namely space-time. But at every stage our penetrating gaze must be fixed on creation, on things human and material, cosmic and earthly, so that the work itself shall partake of the four-fold unity and our picture become a likeness of the whole.

We should have noticed, incidentally, that the pure representation of measurement points towards another realm as yet unknown to us. For instance on the rhythmic plane. The simple rhythm 1+2 represented in terms of linear measurement looks like this:

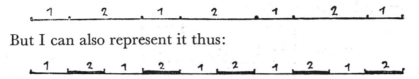

But I can also represent it thus:

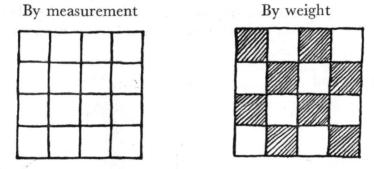

This latter is, however, not a representation of measurement but of weight.

Now transfer this to a two-dimensional surface, and we have the simplest form of weight structure in the chess-board with its alternate squares of black and white.

The division of a surface

By measurement   By weight

If we now transpose that on to the plane of balance and again employ the image of the scales, the following picture results:

Disturbed balance

Measurement

Weight

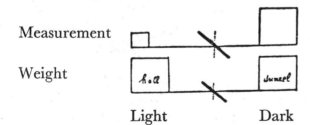

Light   Dark

Corrected balance

Measurement

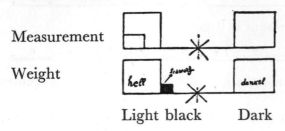

Weight

Light black   Dark

These three little operations with lines, surfaces and scales extend the formal means of measurement and make us familiar with the formal means of weight. That is the plane of tonalities, of chiaroscuro, the most elementary symbol of which is an arrow shaded from white at its base through grey to black at its tip.

Black end

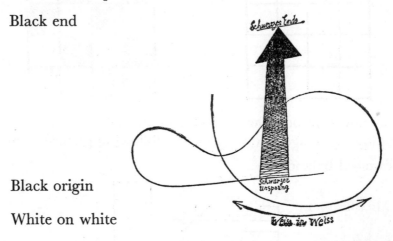

Black origin

White on white

On this new plane all partial operations are governed by the new sign. We have already dealt with line, surface and rhythm. The expansion into the third dimension does not however depend solely on the graduated measurements of perspective, but on the differences of weight produced by

chiaroscuro, which thus creates distance. Similarly, the fourth
dimension—space-time—follows suit and grows out of the
movement produced by the progression from white to black
(or vice versa). And the direction of this movement is determined by an increase in energy, for example, from an inactive
white towards a sudden future action in black.

But the painter is not restricted to black and white; in his
play with light values he can traverse the whole periphery of
the colour circle, that is to say he can produce colour movements through yellow, green, blue and so on. And the operation will be intensified if he traverses the colour circle diagonally, by proceeding from blue through grey to orange, or from
green through grey to red, etc. In so doing he will notice that
the elements of measurement and weight no longer suffice for
the definition of the new formal element—colour. An area of
red is not defined by measurement, although certain of its
elements can be measured; nor is it defined by its weight,
although, for example, if we place a red in our imaginary pair
of scales it will be 'heavier' than blue. Colour is defined by its
quality—red, yellow, blue. On this plane of colour as a quality
all the partial operations have to be gone over again, from a
dot to a line to a plane. The consequent expansion into the
third dimension now results not only through perspectival
measurement and differences in weight between dark and
light, but through the spatial effect of distance created by the
juxtaposition of colours. (For example, areas of colour piled
up and permeating each other, the *'plans superposés'* of Picasso
and Braque). But space-time now develops in the direction of
the movements of colour: in the direction of an increase of
energy (from white rising to green for example);
or in the direction of an increase in light value (from violet to
yellow, for example);

or in the direction of a passage from one complementary to another (from red to green for example);
or in the direction of the warmer colours (from blue to orange for example);
or in the direction of the colder colours (from red to green for example).

These passages from one quality to another produce the mobile factors of the colour composition (the '*sens giratoire*' of Delaunay). But the organism itself demands a higher form of development. 'As norm for such a composition we may postulate: a harmonization of the elements towards an independent, calm-dynamic, or dynamic-calm entity. This composition can only become complete if movement is met by counter-movement, or if a solution of infinite mobility has been found.' The arrows of direction disappear and come to rest in a higher order. And the symbol of this calm-dynamic state in the domain of colour is the spectral colour circle, 'where all arrows are superfluous, because the problem is no longer "to move over there", but to be "everywhere", and hence also "there".'

Now for the wider perspective opened up by the words of Cézanne: 'Nature is not only on the surface, but also in depth; colour is the expression of this depth on the surface, and has its roots deep in the world.'

The pictorial image exists on three levels, and I would like here to quote Klee's summary: 'Measurement is the distinguishing feature of the element line, weight of the element chiaroscuro, quality of the element colour; the formal means of measurement, of weight, of quality, are all fundamentally different but nevertheless reveal certain common characteristics. Colour is quality, weight and measurement. Chiaroscuro is weight and measurement. Line is only measurement. All three meet in the realm of pure colour.' In these dimensions of the pictorial means alone is it decided 'whether pictures or something else will be born'. For everything which can happen or be expressed in art—dream, idea, fantasy—'is only to be taken really seriously if it unites with the proper plastic means and becomes a figuration. If we are fully in control of our means we can be sure of representing things so solidly that even dimensions outside those we are consciously aware of can be reached'.

Certainly—but do not let us exaggerate. Construction is a good thing but it is not everything. Questions of form are decisive for artistic clarification, but even they are not everything. If they are worked out purely we are impelled towards the essential, 'towards the functional rather than the impressive. One learns to catch hold of things by their roots, to see what goes on underneath them, and one learns the prehistory of the visible.' Nevertheless even this is not yet art of the highest order. 'In the highest order mystery intervenes. Intuition is not to be supplanted. Genius cannot be trained.' Here everything is at stake, the unity of the four-fold structure —human and material, cosmic and earthly. 'Classes should be held on holidays, away from the school buildings, out-of-doors under trees, with animals, on rivers or on mountains, in the sea.' For when things pass into the pictorial dimension the miracle occurs of discovering a reflection of nature in its entirety. Everything experienced or seen is translated into the language of art, into quite another, quite transformed and yet quite real world. 'Nothing less is involved if Nature is to be re-born.'

Chapter VII

WAYS OF STUDYING NATURE

If Nature is to be re-born! Does this bring us back by another path to the original biological function of painting—the recreation of the exterior world of man? Only in a comparative sense—and then in an extension of the dimension of seeing, in an extension of the conception of the possibilities of art in relation to Nature. This extension of the dimension of seeing brings to mind other words such as 'looking', 'contemplating' or 'visual experience'. They define what happens rather more profoundly, and so our extended conception becomes art because we are making our impressions visible and revealing certain dark visual images. These are, of course, vague words, but they are only intended to enlarge our understanding of what is happening. Our point of departure must be Klee's surprising comment: 'Communion with nature is for the artist a *condition sine qua non.*'

Let us look at another picture by Klee, a water colour. It is called '*Fishes*' and dates from 1921. This enchanting picture, the colours of which are gentle and subdued, is full of silent movement. Is it a glimpse into an aquarium? At the bottom are some massive, juicy, static vegetable forms, painted light yellow and ochre, which are growing in front of a blue-black background. They are sharply differentiated from each other.

First come stiff, flat upright forms, with sharp edges, like reeds. Next to these, growing out of a soft, grassy bed is an oval formation which produces an elongated form like a bud. Beside this is a second and very similar growth, though larger and better armed, with sharp spikes; its bud has already opened into a broad, pale, fat bloom. To the right of this are other forms with a more crystalline growth. These are growing out of a square base composed of several triangles, and this triangular rhythm develops gently upwards and inwards, as if it might be seaweed pushing up through mud and flint and emerging in geometrical forms. The closer we look, the more familiar we become with this formal vegetation of waterplants, of succulents. We even think of what we would like to call these objects, although the names that come to mind are more biological than descriptive. And although none of these descriptions may be valid in the 'real' sense, we do not doubt that in actual fact these plants might exist somewhere, perhaps in another medium. They have a 'natural', close, warm familiarity. They are variations on natural growths, yet as examples of the formative process they are also part of nature. Immediately above this vegetation we perceive the fishes, their colours changing prismatically, from red-violet through grey-violet to white. Each has a movement of its own which has been elegantly incorporated into the decoration of the sheet. The white circles of their eyes 'nail' the whole thing together in a sensitive arrangement, producing a happy balance, which sets our spirit at rest and starts it thinking. And in the process of thinking these fishes become natural and familiar. Their species too seem to be identifiable, and as old friends we feel like calling them by their names. But it won't quite happen; they seem familiar all right, but we can't find the correct name in our piscatorial vocabulary. Yet it is all just like

Nature. Indeed it is Nature, only taken a little further than usual. We might say that these plants and fishes have been made from the same form-ciphers as occur in marine biology. Obviously, therefore, if one has once encountered these form-ciphers in Nature and seen through them, one can invent quite new kinds, which might also exist.

Everything, it seems, depends on 'seeing through'. Now the first distinctive characteristic that everybody noticed about Klee was the fact that he was all eyes, that all one saw were his great, brown, Bedouin eyes. The eye was for him 'the meeting place of many roads', the starting-point of all images. The whole man was dominated by his obligation to see. Klee could not dispense with Nature. Seeing, contemplating, musing, such were for him the sublime sensations. And he would lose himself in thought at the spectacle of a ray of sunshine skimming over the bark of a tree-trunk, or of shadows playing along the posts of a fence and creating a rhythm. Now Klee backed up his observation of nature with scientific knowledge; he studied anatomy, he collected and pressed flowers in order to find out about their shape, and he watched animals. He referred to this practice as 'finding his bearings among the things of nature and daily life', and he was motivated by a sense of poetic dedication, which came from his very heart. He might suddenly see the quivering shadow cast by a spider in the silvery light of the moon. He would pick the animal up, and wonder whether it could really see its own shadow and whether its life-force was entirely derived from darkness. Then Klee might turn to his visitor and say: 'The shadow of an object is only the memory of its hidden existence, of its origin.' He loved birds, and was excessively fond of cats and snakes which, like the Egyptians, he associated with all sorts of mythical attributes. Klee's white angora cat was for him an Oriental prince in disguise, or even his 'Ka', which roamed the wide world. Klee renounced his youthful delight in fishing because he did not want to kill any living thing. Then there were all the little things which could be observed for hours on end and were best understood through contemplation. He retired with these into his studio: skeletons of small animals, mosses, bark and lichen, shells and stones, beetles and butterflies. They were, literally, most carefully selected, for if one can see through them and master the laws governing their existence and their form, nature itself becomes transparent, the spirit moves and the artist feels impelled to attempt similar acts of formal creation.

Among the early entries in Klee's diaries, in 1902 and 1903 for example, when Klee was still a student, we find references to the importance of working from the nude, but in such a way that 'everything essential, even those vital things which are concealed by optical perspective, are brought out'. Klee attended anatomy classes with medical students in order 'to be able to make new use of the knowledge of the functional mechanism of the body when confronted with a living model'. For 'the embarrassment of the untrained student when confronted with Nature is easily explained; he sees only the outermost branches and cannot see through to the tree-trunk. It is not yet clear to him, as it is to an experienced man, that precise analogies for the laws which govern the existence of the whole are repeated in the smallest outermost leaves.'

Now when Klee was teaching, he was continually asking his pupils what they could see. He did not tell them to look at Nature in order to practise making pictorial generalizations about appearances. Instead he forced them to be very exact in their observation, so that even the most summary look at nature became a real visual study, and thus they could attain that new power which is so essential to an artist: the power of perceptive judgment. The breath of life is concealed in small details, it is deep within. So he made them draw the reflections in a glass of water, or a needle in a small ball of wool; one day he made them copy the armour worn by Grünewald's St. Mauritius, on another a piece of birch bark, or a finely veined

Playful Water, 1935

leaf. These drawings all had to be done so precisely that the object could almost be 'lifted off the page'. For accuracy of observation was the first indication of perceptive amazement, and only those who have known this can experience the formation of natural images within themselves and attain to that elemental realm whence they must draw the nourishment for their own creations. 'Lead your students to Nature, into Nature!' was his advice to a fellow-art teacher (H. F. Geist). 'Let them learn by experience how a bud is formed, how a tree grows, how a butterfly opens its wings, so that they will become as rich, as variable, as capricious, as Nature herself. Perception is revelation, it is an insight into the workshop of creation. That is where the secret lies.' And to a painter his advice was: 'Follow the ways of natural creation, the becoming, the functioning, of forms. That is the best school. Then perhaps, starting from nature, you will achieve formations of your own, and one day you may even become like Nature yourself and start creating.'

Here we find again the expression 'like Nature', which came to us spontaneously while we were looking at the water-colour called '*Fishes*'. What is meant here by 'like'? On the lowest level, no more than a comparison, no more than a listening-in to Nature, so that in a picture one can use her inventions in the way she herself uses them. Klee gave an example of this during one of his lessons. 'The process of "flowing",' he said, 'can be very well observed in the sand on the sea-shore. The caressing air has a part in it, driving it into large and small waves. The receding water at ebbtide leaves its mark of "flowing" with amazing delicacy and firmness. One sees here linear and plastic images, which represent the conception of "flowing".' Now one can allow these images to come to the surface by analogy with Nature, if the pictorial intention requires it. But one must also have an insight into the formative processes of nature, and one must work from this insight not from the varying images which trouble the retina of the eye.

At this point, the language of painting, what happens on the formal plane, comes into its own, for it is on that plane that whatever has been seen and felt of Nature's formative processes is translated into pictorial signs, changed, and thus communicated. Receptivity changes to productivity. The artist who had thought of Nature as a matter of critical selection, now faced the open book of Nature and had to act. Looking at water flowing by he now sees a pictorial formula: surfaces formed of lines moving towards each other. A blossoming apple-tree=a structure of growth. A sleeping man=a structure of functions at rest. A shoal of quivering fishes swimming in a stream, become 'spatial images full of energy with a hint of a third dimension'. This can be explained by looking at the drawing 'Fish in the Brook' of 1926. The swirling, rushing water of the stream is suggested by purely linear means, and within this web are caught the tense, vital bodies of the fishes energetically asserting their existence. Water and animal, flowing and struggling, diving and soaring, element and will.

Klee's experience of natural objects was profound, and always seen in relation to picture-making. Out of seeing came insight, and out of this insight, he made pictorially concrete objects. As an artist, he experienced Nature as a 'powerful opposition', which prevented his image from falling into decoration.

Thus Klee surpassed reality in the sense that he penetrated it critically and transposed it on the plane of the pictorial means. While creating a picture he moved parallel to Nature. So he found himself deeply involved in the pictorial quest of our century. Did not Cézanne say that 'Art is a harmony parallel to Nature'? And any French painter of to-day, Matisse or Picasso, for instance, might well say something similar. This phrase sums up the attitude of mind which is common to the artists of our period, but it has implications of its own which give it additional meaning. In some observations about colour written by the Swiss painter Giovanni Giacometti, for example, occurs a passage where he says that it is essential to

THE MOUNT OF THE BULL, 1923
Private Collection

get behind the colours on the surface of nature 'in order that with the aid of these laws the artist can create an organism which will be parallel to the outer world in all its parts yet as true as nature within itself'. And among the German Expressionists we find Nolde saying: 'My aim was that colours should be transmitted to the canvas, through myself as the painter, with the same inevitability as when Nature herself is

Fish in the Brook, 1926, *Private Collection, Munich*

creating forms, just as minerals and crystals are formed, just as moss and seaweed grow.' These examples will perhaps serve to set us thinking.

Now Klee was always wanting something more, to see still further behind appearances, to draw a little closer to the heart of creation. For him, art was not simply parallel to creation; it was also a simile revealing it. Nature: 'That is the art of Someone Else, but it is an instructive example when we are attempting to realize something analogous with the formal

117

elements of pictorial art.' From this we can now pass on to his saying: 'Just as a child while playing imitates us, so we while playing imitate those forces which have created and which continue to create the world.'

What humanity, what sort of faith inspires such an utterance? For it means nothing less than that what is buried and what is still unborn can be divined in the world around us, that we can lead a life in other mediums, at the bottom of the sea for example, in the air, or in cosmic spheres. Where is the view-point from which all this becomes visible? In 1916 Klee referred to it as his 'own standpoint': 'I love animals and all sorts of unearthly beings dearly. I do not condescend towards them, nor do I elevate them up to my level. Rather do I sink myself beforehand in the universe and then stand in a brotherly relationship to my neighbours, to everything on this earth. I seek a remote point of original creation, where I feel that there is one invariable formula for man, animal, plant, earth, fire, water, air and all directive forces.' (It is that mysterious point, to which secretly all modern thinkers aspire! André Breton for example has written: 'Everything leads us to believe, that a spiritual point exists, where life and death, reality and imagination, past and future, the communicable and the incommunicable, height and depth cease to appear as contradictions.' And Kafka: 'From a certain point there is no more turning back. This point must be reached.') Now Klee's observations were prompted by consideration of the work of Franz Marc. Klee saw that Marc's dominant theme was inspired by a profound spiritual doubt: 'Is this world, which convention has taught us to see, the only possible world? How does an animal see the world for instance? Clearly Marc was asking whether all living things are not bound together in one great unity. Marc tried to find an answer to this, and because he had a deep and questioning love of creation he attempted to discover forms and colours which correspond symbolically to that knowledge of the secrets of the world's unity which lies deeply buried within us. Marc's conception was Franciscan —the *ordo caritatis*, whose agent is love. Klee found something different in himself. His more restless spirit was attracted towards the free elements—'a butterfly hovering in the stellar orbit', Nolde once called him—so he attempted to free himself from warm earthly attachments and lose himself in ever greater mobility. He adopted an attitude slightly opposed to that of Marc, and forsook the love-warmed realm of earth. 'Terrestrial thoughts give way to universal thoughts. Love is remote and religious. Mankind in my work is not a species but a cosmic point.' Man was thus enabled to move to other spheres and could become for instance 'a creature on a star among many other stars'. The arrow is aimed upwards, but from up there something is also aimed back at us.

Klee's idea of the complete interdependence of the universe, a state of affairs which should be verifiable with special organs, gains increasing probability in the earthly sphere, in life and nature. Many threads lead directly to the idea already enunciated by Novalis, that man is perhaps not an isolated being, but a little part or an organ or even only a parasite of some greater being, called the world. Thus man and his relationship with his surroundings would be zoologically comparable with those of the ant, for an ant too does not and could not exist in isolation, because the whole antheap is the animal. This zoological image should suffice to indicate how our own life is bound up in a greater whole. It may even suggest something else, namely that in the smallest particle of nature we can find echoes of the universal design. Thus the secret of the whole universe permeates us also; indeed it can only be found in ourselves by ourselves. Here the arrow is aimed downwards, but from there too it is aimed back at us.

Now can this 'secret' of the spiritual realm be identified? Only as a state of happiness, as a mood, as an awareness of complete harmony between the Self and the world, as Valéry describes it in '*Mon Faust*'. Suggestion or knowledge—we are already almost living in the world of ideas, in that world in fact of which Klee (but also Kafka, Valéry, Breton and others) speaks. That is the point where no division exists between men and objects, where the division between the Self and reality (which Gottfried Benn calls the 'destiny neurosis of the West') no longer exists. At this point, Klee's humanity, which was the mainspring of his art, intervened in the form of conviction, knowledge or knowing belief. His pictures are communications of this state.

Klee was a painter; his organ of sensation and transmission was the eye. Everything had to be taken in through his eye and to come out through it into the picture. His human attitude determined his way of seeing, and consequently this meant total seeing. 'An element of totality enters into our conception of natural objects.' What does that mean? Paul Klee has demonstrated the answer neatly in his own way in a schematic drawing which accompanies his essay '*Ways of Studying Nature*' (in *Staatliches Bauhaus Weimar: 1919–23*.) This makes it clear that the relationship between artists and objects (the 'I' and 'Thou') in the days of Naturalism and Impressionism was optico-physical through the atmosphere. The result was a series of magnificent pictures of the surfaces of objects filtered through light. But now that we have discovered that man is a creature who belongs to a greater unity, this way of seeing is inadequate. 'The object expands beyond its appearance by virtue of our knowledge of its inner workings.'

This knowledge comes to us: (1) *in material ways*, through the dissecting knife and optical instruments (microscope and telescope); (2) *in intuitive ways*, through our power of perceptive judgment, which enables us to see through the outside to the

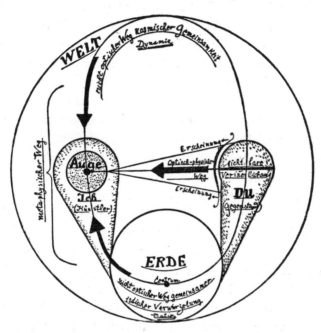

inside of things. Here the process can be reversed by the looking-glass relationship between Individual and Object, so that things inside ourselves are suddenly illuminated by external impressions. (An excellent example of this is Marcel Proust's description of his experience with the church towers of Martinville). This perceptive judgment leads to experiencing, to tuning-in to objects, to assimilating them into our whole attitude to the world. Two paths lead to this humanizing of objects: 1. The non-visual one of common earthly roots, which finds its way into the eye of the 'self' from below. (Rilke has

written: 'The whole society of objects and mankind has with-
drawn into those communal deeps from which the roots of
every living thing draw nourishment'); 2. The non-visual one
of cosmic community, which comes as inspiration from above.
Thus mankind and objects, the earthly and the cosmic, are
fused at the cross-roads of the eye. Once again then we are in
the presence of that four-fold unity which we have met
before. But now we can see Klee's humanity more clearly
as the centre of the circle. His schematic drawing becomes an
impressive symbol of his world-outlook. And if we may borrow a phrase from Heidegger, we might describe this symbol,
in which the division between the Individual and Reality
(this 'destiny-neurosis of the West') is non-existent, as the
quintessence of the four-fold unity.

For the painter, all these paths meet in the eye 'and lead
outwards from their meeting-place, translated into form, to
the synthesis of outward seeing and inward perception. This
meeting-place is the origin of hand-made images which may
be absolutely different from the visual image of an object and
yet, in terms of total vision, do not contradict it. . . . As the
painter learns to observe and look deeply into nature he finds
that the more he aspires to a conception of the universe the
more he is able to indulge in the free creation of abstract
images which go beyond something deliberately schematic
and achieve a new naturalism, the naturalism of the picture
itself. Then he has created something which is parallel to the
work of God'.

The point is that 'Art is parallel to creation; it is at times an
example, just as things terrestrial can be examples of things
cosmic'. Its parallelism is to be found in the quintessence
of the four-fold unity. Klee's whole effort was directed to
repeating the act of creation within himself, in order to reach

Plants, for Earth and Air, 1920

an understanding of the Whole. With this understanding he then set out to create images which fit into and complement the quintessence of the Whole by the fact of being themselves newly created. So Klee could not reproduce Nature. Nature is in him, he is himself Nature. She has been given into his hands; she permeates his whole being. Thus she can express

123

herself rhythmically, as movement and action, or as physical sensation, or even in such an abstract way as in the arabesques executed by a dancer.

Now let us look back at '*Fishes*', and we shall see them with other eyes. Are we perhaps ashamed of our comparison with an aquarium, since the picture does not represent a visual experience? Rather let us say that here a man has moved into another medium, has gone down to the bottom of the sea and is existing there. He knows about it; it permeates him, and then to his astonishment he sees this world growing inside himself. As he goes on working he finds himself on brotherly terms with these terrestrial neighbours. Something flowed towards him from the elemental realm of Nature. It started in the depths, went right through him, became charged with memories of things seen, when once upon a time he repeated creation in himself, and finally became manifest in this image. In front of this little poem about the life, ways and death of fishes we are overwhelmed by that pantheistic piety which we always feel when our self is in harmony with the world. Now perhaps we can see that even this little picture sustains the idea of a parallel to the work of God.

Klee saw a parallel between the way the artist finds his way through life and adjusts himself to nature, and the roots of a tree. 'From the root the sap flows to the artist, flows through him, through his eye.' He turned back to creation, in order to understand its sequence as a whole. Very soon therefore he left the visible world behind him and penetrated to the quintessence of the Whole. Here he worked upon Nature and lost himself in her. He saw through her with his penetrating gaze, experienced and comprehended her—and then he turned away from her and resumed his own serious game. For the world we see is not the realm in which pictures are born.

BIRD-GARDEN, 1924
Collection Ibach, Munich

MOUNTAIN CARNIVAL, 1924
Klee Foundation

Chapter VIII

A PICTURE IS BORN

... then he turned away from her? 'The artist abandons the world immediately around him and instead builds a bridge into another world which is supposed to be complete.'

This was not a conception which originated with Klee. Delacroix already regarded Art as a means of crossing the solid bridge of Nature and reaching a realm where objective forms become hieroglyphs. And without much difficulty we could trace the same idea, in broad outline, in the writings of the German Romantics (Schlegel, Runge etc.). Through them it reached France (the influence of the Hegelian metaphysic was decisive) and Gérard de Nerval's '*Supernaturalisme*' was virtually a programmatic formulation of it. From there it goes straight to the Symbolist movement—and the anti-naturalism of to-day, after which the image of man no longer appears static, but is instead variable, unstable, more that of a transitional than a localized being in the sense of Hermann Hesse's man who 'is no other than the narrow, perilous bridge between Nature and spirit'. Here too there is an echo of Delacroix.

The artistic practice which developed out of this conception does not disregard natural appearances; it merely takes the inherent formal and spiritual possibilities of nature and develops them to the point of clarification. The result is Nature elaborated, stylized (Preraphaelitism, Symbolism, Jugendstil), and spiritually intensified (Romanticism, Naturalism, Expressionism). Thus a long line of artists connect Klee with the Romantic movement to which he was deeply attached.

But in Klee's work there is no direct link with visual images. These he rejected in favour of developing a procedure of his own. 'The artist has to paint quite differently, he must construct forms with quite different terms of reference. The visible world is behind him, he has assimilated it, has sunk himself in it. He has exhausted all that there is to see of the visible world and must advance towards his picture. He transcends reality, dissolves it, in order to reveal what lies behind and inside it.'

The artist 'must advance towards his picture!' Klee's words mean that it is time to stop investigating natural objects, that all this knowledge must be forgotten, and that the artist must free himself of any conscious objective purpose before starting on the construction of his picture on the formal plane. Then he will find that he is able to choose which pictorial elements he wants from the dimensions of measurement, weight and quality (line, tonality, colour), in order to build his new organism, and will be able to fashion an image that will grow logically into his construction. This initial choice is the first productive step, the decisive act, and as such is of course completely involved with feeling, mood, sensation and thought,— in short, with the vital forces predominating at this moment of creation. The source 'whence' the impulse has come remains for the moment obscure; it is only important to know 'what' happens to the picture. The point of departure will only be discovered when the end has been reached. 'The painter knows a great deal, but he only knows it subsequently.'

A PICTURE IS BORN

This can be explained by studying one of Klee's pictures. Let us look at a water-colour of 1925 without knowing its title. The background is deep purple, nocturnal; something is happening in the middle which makes the colours around the edges more radiant, reddish-brown. It proceeds from cold, changes to warm and achieves a velvety, glowing lightness of tone. The lightening process is very gradual. The transitions are gentle, but become very intense as the movement rises from dark-cold to light-warm. This gradual transition is achieved by a special technique of colour-spraying, which was frequently used by Kandinsky as well as Klee during their years together at the Bauhaus. This spraying process is done with cut-outs, that is to say, parts of the picture are covered with bits of shaped cardboard. The mechanical appearance of the outlines, so different from those drawn by hand, is emphasized in this imprecise medium. The upper and lower parts of the picture are composed of forms with precise contours, a structure of rectangles which set up a gentle rhythm. It is a kind of rhythmical network—quiet, static, square after square —that looks as though it would like to extend across the whole picture, this gentle movement being created by answering accents of colour: blue, grey-brown, purple, cloudy white, Naples yellow. The structure of rectangles glows through the dark, warm colour medium and gets lighter in tone towards the top. It is as though a ghostly light were being held up in the dark on some scaffolding: the structure is static and of the utmost simplicity, it is accomplished, built, and standing on the ground. But in this ghostly light it cannot really expand in space. Its physical reality is denied right up to the edges, because the only spatial effect is created by tonal values and colours conditioned by the ghostly light, so even this effect is flat. But from the hard outlines of the structure of rectangles

127

there is a leap into purple darkness, where space and forms are open, where everything is silent. This is a leap into another element, where nothing is accomplished, nothing has form, and nothing stands on the ground. This is a setting for things which happen in dimensions which are quite different from the terrestrial one in which the rectangles are laboriously accumulated. Something is happening in this silent dimension: a bright circle of light has appeared and is rising. It is the source of all the light—the corresponding square of light below makes this immediately apparent—and as it pushes upwards it opens a path for itself through the structure of rectangles which is doing everything to conceal it. Light shining forth and a path leading upwards: a planet is rising. Such is indeed the subject of this picture, for Klee called it 'Moonrise'.

Now how did Klee achieve this? He took the elements of colour and rhythm out of their comfortable resting-places and set to work with them, building and arranging, cutting out stencils and patiently inserting his rectangles into the structure. And while he was arranging the pictorial elements, thinking only of the structure and not consciously intent on anything, he found himself gradually confronted by a picture, by a picture which had been stored within himself and which corresponded to some experience, although hitherto it had had no shape and had existed vaguely in the realm of feeling and memory. This picture was fighting to be born. It troubled him and he had to discover the way to it. He had to journey into the unknown in order to find a way of making visible a disquieting and nameless thing which was hidden within himself. And because his search was successful we can now discover his starting-point: a memory of something profoundly observed and experienced, something that had sunk deep in-

MOONRISE, 1925
Private Collection, Munich

INSCRIPTION, 1926

Guggenheim Foundation, New York

side him but which could be suddenly brought to the surface again as a picture through his way of handling coloured forms. It was a sort of lyrical process running parallel to the creative process. Klee discovered his picture, but it was not until the end that he identified its content, and then he added a descriptive title.

The title, the description, was the last thing to be added. So we must remember that he did not have it in mind beforehand. Klee had no pre-conceived intention. It gave him 'pleasure to add something or other to what was being created, to strengthen an accent or to insist on a direction, in order to link it together, to clarify, classify, purify, reveal, emphasize, weaken, strengthen, activate or suppress'. He went on arranging and building, always with a view to improving and completing his construction, then an image appeared without any intention on his part to represent a particular object or arrive at a specific content. The artist is no more than a mouthpiece and is forced to obey the rules of the pictorial means. He must surrender entirely to the surface which is being painted without seeking to impose some pre-conceived picture upon it. He seeks the laws which govern the birth of pictorial forms and then employs them; he seeks free forms, links, and arrangements in his own way, allowing forms to come into existence on their own. These forms are in no way burdened with an objective content. They are independent images with a life of their own, forms among other forms. They happen, and take their place in a general scheme, as a result of control on the formal plane.

This self-denying way of handling the pictorial means is 'like writing something which strives to become visible. We do not always know at once what flows into us from the elemental realm of Nature, what comes up from the depths and goes through us in order to become manifest in images'. That is what we must discover. It comes out of its own accord, suddenly striking a chord in us while we are working with coloured forms: a memory, an association, the 'Eureka' of recognition! 'However, sooner or later an association may come to mind in the artist. Then nothing will prevent him from accepting it if it presents itself with a very convincing name . . . sometimes one is even very glad if a familiar face appears in a picture as though of its own accord. The objects in pictures look at us gaily or seriously, with more or less intensity, consolingly or frighteningly, with suffering or with a smile. They confront us with every variation in the psychic-physiognomical domain from comedy to tragedy.' And so finally the picture-making conception coincides with a spontaneous poetic conception, though it may now seem to us superficial to describe this coincidence as 'accidental'.

The thought is poetic. It cannot therefore be described with the literalness characteristic of the titles of most paintings: '*The Oath of the Horatii*' or '*The Stone-breakers*' or '*Meadow with Cows*'. A poetic metaphor must be found, because there is nothing in the picture which is known by a name in the visible world; on the contrary, this is something which has only just become visible and is seeking an appropriate name. So the title takes its place on the picture as a verbal comment and a concluding poetic metaphor. And Klee was a fine poet. He could always think of something. Hence his titles: '*Garden of the Passions*', '*Death for an Idea*', '*Fool in a Trance*', '*Saint of the Inner Light*', '*Mount of the Bull*', '*Juggler in April*', '*Numerical Trees*', '*Growth of Nocturnal Plants*', '*Silver Moon Chimes*', '*Scholar conversing with Planets*', '*Dream Bird*', etc. Titles such as these conjure up most poetically the parallel realm of action in which the image exists and reveal the emotional point whence it originated. They are the sort of titles Morgenstern loved to invent, and it is worth noting that Klee first came across the *Galgenlieder*, (which were published in 1905) in 1910. Titles of this sort began to be given to pictures when direct objective speech had been discarded and the tissue of colours and forms was allowed to speak softly but firmly for itself. Thus they were used by the Symbolists. Gauguin entitled a picture of a recumbent nude Tahitian girl '*Manao Tupapau*' (The Spirit Watches). And he chose for the title of one of his large figure compositions '*Whence do we come? Who are we? Whither are we Going?*' Now Gauguin described the origins of this picture and its title in a letter of 1899 to Fontainas: 'The idol is there not as a literary explanation but as a statue, less statue perhaps than the animal shapes; less animal too, embodying my dream in front of my hut with nature entire reigning in *our primitive soul*, imaginary consolation for our sufferings in what they contain of the hazy and misunderstood before the mystery of our origin and our future. And all this is chanting mournfully in my soul and my surroundings, as I paint and dream at the same time, without an apprehensible allegory in my reach. On awakening, my dream ended, *I said to myself:* Whence do we come? Who are we? Whither are we going? A reflection which is no longer part of the canvas, but was written just as I said it on the wall surrounding the canvas, not a title therefore but a signature.'

If we now consider Klee's circle of friends, we shall find that Franz Marc too attempted to suggest the super-objective implications of coloured forms by poetic metaphors. Such titles as the following occur in his work about 1912–13: '*The Poor Land of Tyrol*', '*Tower of the Blue Horses*', '*The Cosmic Cow*', '*The Trees showed their Rings and the Animals their Veins*', '*The First Animals*', '*Magic Moment*', '*Workshop for Creation*'. The more a picture overstepped the limit of reality, the more insistently the coloured forms began to speak for themselves; hence the explanation of its content had to be more elaborate, more poetic, more metaphorical, until the title became simply an indication. Klee adopted this system. He wanted to make a communication and was not prepared (he attached great importance to this) to accept a mere formal arrangement which demanded no title and could be labelled—like many of Kandinsky's pictures—simply 'Composition' or 'Improvisation'.

Klee took what was given to him, but as soon as he recognized the image that was evolving he embellished it with poetry. 'The spectator explains, sees lines, surfaces, chiaroscuro and colours which awake memories in him. But it is the interrelation of the parts which produces the meaning. I am in the end a spectator myself and accept what falls into my lap.' Klee became a spectator of his own work in order to discover its content; his images suggested their own designation. 'Acceptance of this objective association then provokes this and that addition which must have some inevitable connection with the object in question.'

Klee was a tireless worker, but he knew that one must be patient with an image if it is to yield up its meaning. He was busy all day at his work-table, scraping, priming, spraying, dabbing, scratching, drawing or hanging up damp sheets of water-colour on a line to dry. All around his studio, on easels and on the walls, were pictures, some begun, some half-finished or almost finished, but each with its own troubles and demands. Klee moved among them like a magician, going from one to another listening attentively to the requests of each. And this ability to listen sympathetically and understand at once was also typical of his human relationships. A work of art was to him a becoming, it was like a plant which was growing to maturity, the outcome of a constant activity directed towards higher things. He himself was only the medium, through which the image grew. 'A thing in course of forming becomes visible as a figuration.' This figuration then demands a name, to prove that it has transferred itself from the region of the unknown into that of the familiar and the known. Sometimes therefore Klee would come upon a title when talking with friends about his pictures, but equally he might adopt a title suggested by someone else if it seemed particularly appropriate. This process he referred to as 'christening his pictures'.

Reduced to its simplest terms, this means no more than that Klee was able to read something objective into any combination of forms. Now it is well known that one has only to stare at an old wall, for example—and there is no need for it to be a wall pregnant with historical or mythological connotations, such as the walls of Crete, of Tarquinia or of Peru—in order to lose oneself in absent-minded contemplation, induced, one knows not how, by a sort of visual hallucination. At such times the aesthetic sensibility is unusually alert, though we do not know exactly why. Now, since man is always trying to assimilate everything spiritually, his power of imagination comes into play at this point and he begins to discover an objective significance in the cracks, lumps and stains before his eyes. Suddenly he sees pictures appearing on the wall, and these pictures are projections of himself, because his imagination reflects his state of mind, his mood, that is to say something in his unconscious. Modern psychology makes great use of this sort of procedure. But painters have long been familiar with it. The extent to which pre-historic cave paintings may have been based on explanatory additions to natural markings on the walls is still uncertain. But we have better established historical evidence. Leonardo, for example, told his pupils to look at cloud-formations and try to see something objective in them. And Piero di Cosimo saw wonderful pictures in drink-stains on the walls of Florentine taverns. Sung-Ti, a Chinese painter of the eleventh century, maintained that landscapes could be discovered in the damp-stains on the walls of bamboo huts: this, he said, was a 'heaven-sent' not an 'earthly' inspiration.

Not earthly, but 'heaven-sent'—these are remarkable words. Yet like all things oriental they have a profound meaning. They refer to that secret magic which anything accidentally discovered, anything which appears mysteriously, has for man. Hermann Hesse says, in *Weg nach Innen*, that if searching implies an aim then finding means 'to be free, to be open, to have no aim'. Here one is reminded of Picasso's dictum: 'I do not seek, I find.' All this amounts to in fact is that if we are disinterested and receptive a picture will suddenly appear before our eyes as if by magic. In Klee's own words: 'Remain open through life, much-favoured child, child of creation.' Now the fear and fascination induced by one's own discovery are reflections of that long-forgotten 'magic' power of art which survives in children and 'savages'. For when a 'savage' has carved a fetish he puts it at a distance from himself, studies it with obvious emotion and then bows down before it as though it were something strange and newly discovered in the making of which he has had no part, something which has been placed in his hand by supernatural powers. We know more to-day than we used to about this 'magic', and we can learn more and more if we follow the way to the great Within. Picasso and Masson, Léger and Miró, Baumeister and Mataré know that. Paul Klee followed the same path.

This procedure has been widely applied in modern paint-

ing and it is at the root of much modern artistic theory. We
have seen that, as his own spectator, subject-matter was dictated to Klee by the suggestive power of the colours and forms
of his constructions, and that 'according to the associations
they evoke, these constructions will assume concrete names
such as star, vase, plant, animal, head or man'. Now the same
experience occurred as Cubism passed from the analytical to
the synthetic phase. Juan Gris, the purest and most deliberate
artist of synthetic cubism, has described it at length in his
writings and letters. This is what he wrote to Carl Einstein in
1923:

'It would almost be true to state that, with rare exceptions,
the method of work has always been inductive. The elements
of a concrete reality have been rendered pictorial, a given
subject has been made into a picture. My method of work is
exactly the opposite. It is deductive. It is not picture "X"
which manages to correspond with my subject, but subject
"X" which manages to correspond with my picture. I call
this a deductive method because the pictorial relationships
between the coloured forms suggest to me certain private relationships between the elements of an imaginary reality. The
mathematics of picture-making lead me to the physics of representation. The quality, or the dimensions of a form or a
colour, suggest to me the appellation or the adjective for an
object. Hence I never know in advance the appearance of the
object represented. If I particularize pictorial relationships to
the point of representing objects, it is in order that the spectator shall not do so for himself, and in order to prevent the
combination of coloured forms suggesting to him a reality
which I have not intended. . . . It is, then, by being my own
spectator that I extract the subject from my picture.'

Here let us note how the categories of difference established

135

in logic are applied to pictorial thinking. For the distinction between 'inductive' and 'deductive' made by Juan Gris is founded on Kant. The old Socratic classification of thought processes as 'analytical' (that is to say, starting from a given entity and proceeding to draw conclusions about its individual components) and 'synthetic', (that is to say, starting from the particular and creating the general), was accepted by Kant and renamed 'inductive' and 'deductive'. Now if we apply these to the field of art they will be seen to correspond to the precise formula which Merck taught to the young Goethe. Merck distinguished between two artistic tendencies: the one 'by which a poetic form is imposed on reality' (that is to say the 'inductive', 'analytical' method), the other 'by which the poetic, the imaginary, is made real' (that is to say the 'deductive', 'synthetic' method). The pictorial thinking of our cen-

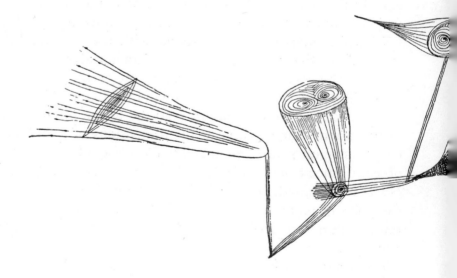

Inclined Blooms, 1927, *Private Collection, Bern*

tury represents the ultimate development of this latter tendency—that is to say, making the imaginary real. Technical
processes and everyday scenes have become the pure pictorial
means in their abstract significance. Through them the picture
becomes visible. This was Gauguin's attitude too. For he maintained that just as a poet first of all hits on a rhythm, so a
painter first sees his image as coloured forms and only subsequently elaborates them with signs—*excitants*—which 'sig-
nify' something objective. Thus Gauguin 'qualifies' a combination of coloured forms in order to turn them into objects.
Juan Gris calls that 'ratifying'. And Cézanne said 'I take
colours and they become objects, without my thinking about
them'. The pictorial construction expresses the origin of the
image and remains its primary content, though it has been
particularized by the addition of objective attributes. Hölzel,

whose theoretical writings also influenced Klee, describes the two methods very exactly: 'If we must learn to develop objects out of simple two-dimensional forms, then we can only transform two-dimensional forms into objective ones by adding objective attributes to them.' Form comes first. 'Form is identical with expression,' says Breton.

An object which becomes visible in this way, that is to say which is discovered or appears by chance, has a special quality. It has the quality of an emblem. It is not a record of things seen, but a sign which has passed through many psychic layers. Juan Gris refers to this sort of emblem. He knew the power they have to express all the perceptual data which cubism in its analytical phase sought to represent simultaneously in a picture. He calls this the 'evocative force of the emblem' and compares it with the *vertu incantatoire* of the groups of words and sounds used by Mallarmé—both have the power of calling up images. With Rimbaud, this magic handling of words is called *alchimie du verbe*. We could even speak of a 'Kabbala of form' such as Ambelain describes: 'Seen from the point of view of tradition it is cabbalistic to assume that, in the "world of sound", two words or two tones, whose harmonies are related, have an undisputed relationship in the "world of pictures".' These two classifications lead us to an esoteric realm, which has hitherto been concealed in secret lore with a demonic or religious bias. In the pictorial sphere, the emblem is endowed with the power to relate the world of coloured forms to that of pictorial content. We find too in history that this power was concealed by esoteric devices: inscriptions on shields with signs which provided the seers with knowledge about the life and death of entire families, religious and magic symbols, alchemists' and astrologers' hieroglyphics, pictographic signs. The abbreviation and concentration of an emblem signifies some past event, it points back to where the secret meaning is hidden. In origin, however, an emblem is the highest common factor of a great number of simultaneous and separate perceptions, ideas and feelings. This is being demonstrated to-day and freed from esoteric fanaticism. The objective discoveries of Klee or Gris have the same evocative powers as an emblem. They originate as new objects, to which nothing in reality directly corresponds; they are the summation of something towards which all automatic pictorial activity is unconsciously struggling. Their challenge gives the spectator a key which enables him to reconstruct the entire genesis of a picture and thus to discover the cause of the original artistic emotion. We 'understand' the image: we receive its message.

I have just used two key-words which describe how a picture is born; 'unconscious' and 'automatic'. These words were fundamental in the vocabulary of the Surrealist movement. Klee never actually joined the Surrealists, though they made free use of his name on their own behalf. When the first Surrealist exhibition opened in Paris, in November 1925, André Breton, the spokesman of the Surrealists, included Klee among the exhibitors. His pictures were hung there beside those of Picasso, Arp, Masson, Ernst, Miró, de Chirico, Man Ray. And the First Surrealist Manifesto, issued by André Breton in 1924, contains a reference to Klee.

Now what is Surrealism? Its aim is to represent what is unconscious, a tendency which has become increasingly favoured by all branches of human science (Medicine, Psychology, Philosophy) since the beginning of this century. Breton's aim, as stated in the Manifesto of 1924, was 'to reconcile the contradiction which has hitherto existed between dream and reality in an absolute reality, in a super-reality'. Thus the

Surrealist turns his back on the visible appearance of the outer world and takes refuge in a magic realm of unreality where man's inner self is revealed in dreams. Yet not only in dreams, for this revelation can occur whenever we suppress the surface consciousness of our senses and thereby release the unconscious stimuli of our inner self. Hallucination, hysteria, trances, every kind of madness, are all regarded to-day as valuable approaches to knowledge. Neuroses are considered worth studying. The Surrealists do not regard poetry and painting as being primarily art-forms, but as ways of researching into that gigantic realm over which pure reason has no control. In order to penetrate this realm, they copied psycho-analysis and resorted artistically to a procedure known as 'psychic automatism'. They made use of the knowledge that the rhythm of words, colours and tones can act like a spell on man and set him dreaming, so that he discovers in himself pictures and symbols of exciting and unknown things by which the unconscious is troubled and which he then communicates and makes comprehensible to us in painting and poetry. Thus Breton describes Surrealism as 'a pure psychic automatism, which sets itself the aim of expressing that which thought dictates, independent of every control by reason'. The unconscious in control: this is a way of communicating the experiences of man's innermost self. Playful, automatic, uncontrolled by reason, this way of handling words, colours and forms carries us to a higher plane where the irrational is at work and where all the symbols and pictorial subject-matter which are hidden in the Unconscious become available. The Surrealist therefore invents nothing but finds everything. He finds profound experiences and profound pictures, which he tries to bring to light through his activity. And there is one assumption which no Surrealist would question. He believes that he is able to penetrate the realm of the unconscious and reach a level at which man himself is Nature, an essential part of the universe. He hopes by this means to break out of the prison of our five senses and to be able to suspend the painful division between individual existence and reality. It is the point at which reality and imagination cease to appear contradictory of which André Breton speaks: 'It would be useless to look for any other motivation behind Surrealism than the hope of determining this point.' For the Surrealist, reality is only to be found in the images and symbols of our inner world; it is to be found therefore in art. So the Surrealist poet Pierre Reverdy could write: 'Reality is those works of art, as yet unborn, which are like crystals in that they are only precipitated after an effervescent and disturbing contact of the mind with something transcendental.'

That sounds familiar, and so it is. For while we were attempting to elucidate the pictorial thinking of Klee, we frequently came across similar statements. There are many similarities between the pictorial thinking of the Surrealists and that of Klee. We can see this, for example, in his curiosity about and interest in naïve and unselfconscious painting— folk art, the art of primitive peoples, the pictures of '*maîtres populaires*', children's drawings and even the doodles of bored art-teachers. Yet Klee belongs to a world of far greater dimensions because he felt himself to be a part of the quintessence of the Whole. He could never have said like Breton: 'The word freedom is the only one which really provokes me.' For he felt quite differently. Klee said: 'My hand is simply a tool which is remotely controlled. It is not my head which functions there but something else, something higher, and more remote, somewhere. I must have powerful friends there, light ones but also dark.' Klee was not concerned simply with recording stimuli from his unconscious. He was not just an *'appareil enregistreur'*, to use Breton's phrase. In fact, there is a hint of reproof in the First Surrealist Manifesto when Breton refers to Klee, Picasso, Braque and some other painters as *'des instruments trops fiers'* who are not content to be simply sounding-boards of the Unconscious. Klee had a mission of his own, and that was 'to make visible as form something which is in process of forming'. The origin of every picture, the place where it germinates, is certainly the 'unconscious'. But this particular 'unconscious' is that of a painter, that is to say an organism which produces pictures. So it is opened wide, cultivated and prepared, a treasure-house of experiences and impressions which have been elaborated and absorbed until they have become absolutely inseparable from the man's personality. This pictorial Unconscious is the store-place of sublime sensations, exalted feelings, delicate attachments, astonishing emotions, memories recaptured and becoming continually more precious. It is a workshop of visible wonders and reassuring experiences concerning the harmony of the world. Now the visible wonders of the world were transmitted to this treasure-house through the eye (aided by the reason and the spirit), and they have been stored up there until they were ripe enough to find their own way out. That was the real meaning of Klee's phrase about 'coming to terms with the things of Nature and of life'. These are specially chosen things, by which our sensibility or our soul were once very much affected and which are preserved until they become a part of the individual personality. That is why Klee's pictorial world is so select, so pure, why it contains nothing abstruse, licentious, sexually passionate, grotesque, insulting or common, nothing in short deriving from those lower depths which are common to us all and which

A PICTURE IS BORN

Freudian analysis has now revealed to us. The Surrealists tell us about these depths, but not Klee. It is not the 'unconscious' that concerns him. He is like some oriental sage who knows intuitively all about the unconscious impulses. He is a painter, and his 'unconscious' is subject to professional discipline; it is enriched through work. 'One must know a great deal and be able to do a great deal, while creating the impression of its being innate, instinctive. Training is important in order to achieve mastery; training of the eye, training of the spirit, training of the understanding.' Everything is filtered, selected and simplified through the power of memory. But 'it is not just a question of the memories themselves. They must first of all get into our bloodstream. For only when their looks and gestures have become nameless and indistinguishable from ourselves can it happen that, at rare moments, the first word of a verse arises in their midst and detaches itself from them'. (Rilke).

It detaches itself from them as the first step towards germination, and then submits to the discipline of the means. Even this method of handling the pictorial means has something to do, in origin, with the 'psychic automatism' of the Surrealists. Something emerges out of darkness and takes form without conscious intention, without direction. It is like a cryptic writing which strives to become visible, to transmit a communication. But here again it must submit to a strict discipline: the process of selection, refinement, fabrication and completion. That is called 'finding one's way on the formal plane'. There the image grows according to the subtle laws of living things. There too is decided whether a picture will be born and also what sort of picture. For there the young seed sprouts, develops according to its own laws of organic growth and comes to the surface as a living and well-formed image.

There we recognize it and interpret the message it brings. Such is the way in which a picture is born: 'From a formative origin, through the discipline of the means to creation.'

Now let us look back again at our picture. It has taken on a new dimension, that of becoming. We can follow the story of its birth because we have learnt to read. Now we can feel something of that creative moment when the first form presented itself simply as a rhythmic construction of cells which wanted to spread in a delicate pattern across the organism of the whole picture. But the growth was checked. The tissue of cells became a rigid construction of rectangles because suddenly the positive constructive impulse was inhibited by the surprising discovery of its negative form. There is something remarkably mis-shapen about it, for only the edges of the rectangles mark, in a negative sense, the various planes. Its spatial limits are not defined. One looks out from the rectangular construction as though into an abyss. This demanded darkness, purple, infinity. Then the picture became nocturnal. Now the rectangles are seen in a light which comes from nowhere and has no form. And these two factors—the formlessness of this dark, endless object which is only negatively present, and the light which comes from nowhere—demanded a decisive act. So Klee allows a new and, with regard to the ensemble of the picture, unique form to emerge out of the spatial darkness—a round disc, which, like something precious or strange, remains spatially isolated from the rectangular forms. It grows out of the darkness, using it as a vehicle and thereby giving it a function and a shape. But the round form must be light and glowing in order to justify the play of light. This decisive act, which assists the whole abstract construction towards its formal completion, immediately produces the objective emblem. At the same time this proclaims its 'evocative

ALL ROUND THE FISH, 1926
Museum of Modern Art, New York

OCEANIC LANDSCAPE, 1929
Private Collection, Munich

power'. The abstract round form is suddenly recognized as a heavenly body, and then the whole picture becomes intelligible. It corresponds to all our private experiences and memories of long-forgotten moonlight nights. We feel poetry stirring within us, and remember the longings which we felt one night as the moon sailed over our house. Nor do we tire of weaving poetic day-dreams around this objective occurrence. Indeed such is the evocative power of this emblem, that it can make visible something universal and typical; it is a form into which have been packed a variety of appearances and experiences. Moonrise! The picture is at one and the same time a wonderful independent creation of our spirit and an hermetic simile for existing things: imago, pictorial seal, emblem, behind which are concealed innumerable tonal echoes of our awareness of the universe. Images of perceptive contemplation, waiting till the emblematic sign pronounces the correct pass-word to release the lock on our tuned-in sensibility and allow us an insight into the new reality of the picture.

It is only possible to turn things into emblems if one knows all about them, has seen them a hundred times, and can no longer distinguish them from oneself. Then they present themselves fully formed as complex signs. New objects we have never seen before, but which nevertheless are complete similes for external reality, which has been changed into an inner reality, which we may call imago, emblem, type or figuration.

But what, pictorially speaking, is an imago?

Chapter IX

THE HEART OF A PICTURE

Frequently words form combinations on their own. The sound-images thus created seem to us to point to secret associations of meaning which are not immediately comprehensible. But if we take the sounds and consider them critically we almost inevitably discover an underlying root-word, in which the sound and the meaning are again united. Speech develops rapidly, pushing out healthy shoots in all directions, and according to the twists and turns of each shoot so it presents a certain picture of appearances to our conscious self and takes on a particular meaning, which entirely obscures the single archaic sense of the original word. Now if we go back from these super-imposed sounds and meanings to the root-word, we find that all the individual meanings unite to form a whole and fill up the gaps. In other words, if we go back to the archaic meaning we shall find combinations of meaning which are denied to us by the subsidiary meanings. Etymology is a fundamental part of all thinking. That is only natural, for the development from the root-word to the subsidiary meanings represents an entire thought-process, and we can only trace the whole of this thought-process if we know where it started. The same applies in botany, where each individual plant has its own scent, its own colour and in-

HIGHWAY AND BYWAYS, 1929

Private Collection, Munich

dividuality, but yet belongs to a whole species, to a plant type, which enables one to recognize individual variations. This is a morphological process, a process of genesis, a process which we must always bear in mind when considering Klee's ideas about picture-making. We said just now that most artists of our century, and Klee in particular, were concerned with making imaginary things real. Then subsequently we came upon the Latin root-word 'imago'. Now if we succeed in understanding this word 'imago' in all its fullness, in all its original significance, we shall discover the sort of picture in which imaginary things are made real. The heart of a picture!

Let us start once more by looking at one of Klee's pictures. It is rather a large oil painting (83 × 67 cm.), called '*High way and Byways*' and was painted in 1929. It was exhibited in 1929 in the 'Sonderbund' Exhibition at Cologne, together with another picture, called '*Necropolis*'. It is related to other pictures of the same period, especially one in an American collection called '*Glimpse of the Land of Plenty*'.

This picture is like a strange wallpaper, composed of small strips and areas of colour close together. In parts the surface is so wrinkled that it looks like dried mud. The dominating colour is sandy yellow, which is made earthy by the presence of ochre, purple and red-brown. There is also a pale green; and between these colours are frequently repeated areas of watery blue. Purely by virtue of their harmony, this watery blue and earthy yellow suggest to us an association of water and earth, while the warm reddish colour suggests something growing and fructifying. The paint is thick, every centimetre of the surface has been worked over, re-touched, or scraped as though the artist were trying to give an absolutely accurate topographical picture of some locality. This feeling of breadth, of topography, becomes more insistent the more one's eye wanders over the picture and becomes familiar with it. There are some hard principal lines, drawn with mathematical precision, though interrupted here and there, which run like paths right across the picture from bottom to top. Our eye is directed along these, and if we allow it to follow these paths we shall see that the feeling of topography is induced by a broad road which runs right across the centre of the picture and diminishes perspectively. Obviously the highway! This road narrows, and we say to ourselves: 'Aha! The thing is seen from above!' So it is like a wide plain which is intercepted at top and bottom by horizontal strips suggesting a river-basin or the banks of a wide river insome primeval valley. That is just what it is. I said that this picture was one of a group of pictures, and mentioned the *'Glimpse of the Land of Plenty'*. There too we see a wide, fertile plain with pyramids in the fore-ground—an unmistakable image of Egypt. On his fiftieth birthday Klee, who had always been profoundly drawn to the Middle East and the Mediterranean—North Africa, Sicily, Egypt—went on a visit to Egypt, and his experience is reflected in a whole series of pictures. Our picture is one of these. It is a pictorial simile for ancient Egypt, for the rich flood-land of the Nile Valley, with its many little fields, yellow and orange under the brilliant sun, its wrinkled but fertile mud, and its patches of pale green where the fields have been laboriously cultivated.

This is not a landscape, let it be said; it is hardly a re-presentational picture. Klee never saw anything like it; the image grew within him, and in the course of his experiments with the pictorial means found its way out. It is a product of the studio, the result of thought and inspiration. Suddenly his carefully planned composition was filled with a wonderful, objective emotion, a sort of vague memory-image which was more a matter of feeling than a clear idea for a picture. Indeed it was not until his hand took control of the pictorial means that his vision materialized, and as the process of composition advanced it became clearer and more visible. It turned into a pictorial image which took the place of the emotion he had felt in front of nature. This picture is therefore not an exact transcription but rather a kind of pictorial metaphor, a formal simile for an existing emotion, which suddenly revealed itself as a dreamy recollection of Egypt. It is a communication—a self-revelation also. Klee the dreamer looked, so to speak, over the shoulder of Klee the painter while he was working and arranging, and both suddenly exclaimed to Klee the conscious human being: 'Look, that's what it was like.' The happiness of rediscovery, the 'Eureka' of recognition! This happiness is locked up in Klee's pictures. But we too can find it, if we have learnt to see through the hermetic structure of the forms.

Franz Marc once said: 'Art is probably a sleep-walker's vision of the typical.' This type of vision is clearly implicit in our picture. Typical elements have been extracted from a landscape and fashioned into a pictorial crystal, whose many facets reflect, the longer we look at them, an image of the actual landscape which produced the original pictorial emotion. Now if we can see what a picture of this kind means, we must know what it is. It is a visual echo which developed in the artist's memory while he was thinking about what he experienced in Egypt—a private sign that contains within itself this typical picture, but which has been produced in the mind of Klee while he was dreaming and composing. Thus the 'sleep-walker's vision of the typical' finds expression in a composite pictorial image: in other words, it takes form.

This image takes form pictorially, after which it attains to the poetic realm of recognition and understanding. If we now apply a saying of Klee's to our picture, we shall be able to follow the various stages: 'A field of young corn is not a field of young corn, but an arrangement of lines, a breath of spring, a carpet over the earth.' By our powers of critical observation we recognize the structure of the image, we then transform and realize it pictorially, and so attain to the realm of poetry, of the imagination. It emerges from there as an effective simile for the forces of the cosmos and the forces controlling this earth. Let me now quote yet another saying of Klee: 'And if finally I allow the unearthly forces to swing far out into the void, I shall surmount the emphatic and impulsive stylistic phase and shall attain a romanticism which merges into the universe.'

Romanticism. That seems an important word, so let us take it seriously and see whether the ideas which we have treated so far have anything in common with the Classical-Romantic antithesis. Besides this is particularly worth doing because, if we succeed in proving that Klee's own word is applicable, then we can answer our own questions about the heart of a picture by Klee with the authority of the great masters of the past. Already we seem to have met with a certain amount of evidence concerning this: words, sayings, ideas, or comparisons which suggested themselves to us from the great realm of Classical-Romantic thought, comparisons with Novalis and Schlegel, with Runge and C. D. Friedrich, with Goethe, and with Carl Gustav Carus, the man most responsible for working over Goethe's ideas in a later generation.

The comparison with Goethe is astonishingly close, for Klee's spiritual development followed a course which was in the main absolutely parallel with that of Goethe. It began early and with very similar experiences. In 1901, when he was twenty-two years old, Klee went to Italy with his school-friend, Her-

FOOL IN A TRANCE, 1929
Private Collection, Wiesbaden

HOVERING, 1930
Klee Gesellschaft, Bern

mann Haller. There, while he was looking at some of the great buildings, he became instinctively aware that 'the visibly calculable relationships of one part to another and to the whole correspond to hidden numerical relationships which govern the form of other artistic and natural organisms'. Such was the origin of Klee's idea that even the purely abstract creations of the human spirit obey the same formative laws as the objective creations of Nature. Goethe was struck by exactly the same experience in front of some of the great buildings of Italy. Indeed he was so struck by it that he referred to this architecture as 'a second Nature serving bourgeois ends'.[1] And he set himself 'to track down the origin of things'[2] so that he could analyse and master his experience that the formative principles which govern natural growth are also the basis of all art. A little later Goethe wrote of the Greek artists: 'I have a suspicion, that they even proceeded in accordance with the laws of Nature and that I am on the track of these.'[3] But if everything that is produced in Nature or in Art derives from the same organizing impulse, then it is essential 'to get very close to the "How" of the productive organism'.[4] Thus, at the Temple of Minerva at Assisi, Goethe marvelled 'that, like Nature, the artists of classical times could come to terms with anything'.[5] That is the only way to produce 'true art, which is as logical as natural objects'. And in front of the aqueduct at Spoleto he recognized that 'these exalted works of art are the greatest natural creations of man and have been produced in accordance with true, natural laws. Everything arbitrary or conceited, must yield. There is necessity, there is God'.[6] After that he spoke of 'Architecture, sculpture and painting being

[1] *Italienische Reise*, Part 1, p. 190.
[2] *Tagebuch*, p. 332.
[3] *Italienische Reise*, Part 1, p. 265.
[4] Ibid., Part 3, p. 66.
[5] *Tagebuch*, p. 209
[6] *Italienische Reise*, Part 3, p. 78.

like mineralogy, botany and zoology'.[1] Now this vision which Klee, like Goethe, experienced through looking at the architecture of Italy, was also described by Schinkel, the most important architect of the Classical-Romantic epoch. 'Architecture', said Schinkel, 'is the continuation of Nature in her constructive activity.' Thus we are forced to recognize that even 'non-representational' art, as represented by architecture, is tied to objective categories and a strict observance of these is the guarantee that the artistic image will be perfect. And this perfection produces its 'naturalism'.

These objective categories do more than lie on top of natural appearances; they are part of the formative processes of Nature herself. As natural forms are critically rejected during the process of becoming, so Nature's own structural laws become evident. Klee was still young when he reached the conclusion that every individual part of nature's complex organism is governed by some structural law and 'that precise analogies

[1] *Tagebuch*, p. 333.

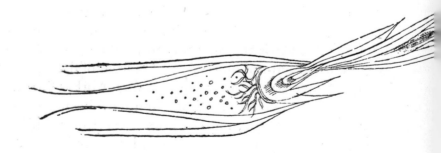

Flying Seed, 1925

for the laws which govern the existence of the whole are repeated in the smallest, outermost leaves'.

Klee realized that in the process of coming to terms with
the world pictorially, he had to extract something typical,

something which could be given form, from the confusion of appearances. 'I suspect that some law is involved, only I must not begin with hypotheses but with an example. . . . And from a series of examples I shall automatically discover what is typical.' What Klee calls 'typical' here refers to the primeval essence of a thing, that form which lies concealed within it. It cannot be seen unless one looks beyond the surface, for an eye that stops at surface appearances ('optical-physical seeing' Klee called this) will only see a schematic projection. But an artist must see 'everything of importance, even those things which are obscured by optical perspective', and must allow them to find their way on to the surface of his canvas. The essential form can only be seen if the eye has that penetrating spiritual power which Goethe (like Kant) calls 'the power of intuitive judgment'. For Klee, the painter, an 'intuitive' result could only be developed through the means of art; for the form as such is not visible, but has to be made visible. 'Art does not reflect what is visible, but makes things visible.' The essential form is born within the artist as he responds to and reflects an object. Through art it is made visible after the artist has experienced a direct emotion and gained a profound insight into the creative processes of Nature.

Goethe's insight was conditioned by his preoccupation with natural sciences, and so he developed it on a literary plane into a morphology of plants. He attempted to put order into the apparent confusion of natural appearances and, relying on his eyes alone, to trace the basic forms underlying all cycles of appearance. His means of recognition was precisely his power of intuitive judgment by which he was able to see through the complexity of things, discover what is typical, and then develop this as form. Form in Goethe's sense stretches forwards and backwards into future and past stages of creative

THE SEALED LADY, 1930
Collection Vowinckel, Munich

HOW IT ALL GROWS! 1932
Klee Foundation

development. Thus it contains within it the idea of the world as genesis, of nature constantly changing and creating. The original form of a plant or an organism is for Goethe the central point of a complex cycle of appearance of similar forms, and with this key—as he wrote to Herder in 1787—'one could go on interminably inventing plants which, even if they do not in fact exist, might well do so without being merely painted or poetic shadows and apparitions, for they would have an inner truth and necessity'. Klee had just the same sort of insight into things—we spoke of it in connection with the water-colour '*Fishes*'—and everything he did or thought was based on the conviction that the will to form is released by the recognition of something underlying appearances, something typical which can be given form, and that it is this which prevents it working arbitrarily. With Goethe as with Klee, we find constant references to the 'genetic treatment', and the 'genetic method', that is to say a gradual advance achieved by critical selection through seeing, contemplating, speculating, analysing, penetrating, and slowly comprehending objects to such an extent that one can spiritually recreate them. Hence the search for the primeval, for original phenomena, for a plant, a stone, or a song, in its original or simplest state. Hence what Goethe, in a letter of 1827, called his 'belief in the continuity of original creation'.[1] These original phenomena represent at the limit of man's possible experience. Indeed they can easily be 'left in their eternal peace and glory'.[2] For behind them lies a world, hidden from us, of which the visible world is only a reflection. Now one of Klee's aphorisms should be set beside these thoughts of Goethe: 'Art is parallel to creation; sometimes it is a sample, just as this earth is a sample of

[1] Letter to Zelter, 29th March 1827.
[2] '*Zur Farbenlehre*: Didaktischer Teil, 177

The Big Dome, 1927

the cosmos.' This hidden something which escapes the enquiring reason will only allow itself to be perceived and reproduced. We can produce this 'essence of reality' in ourselves by means of our power of intuitive judgment. Through his art, 'through studying Nature's continuous process of creation, man can become worthy of participating spiritually in her productions'.[1] He can learn to make productive use of what Goethe, at the age of seventy, called 'The Alphabet of the World Spirit'.[2]

[1] *'Anschauende Urteilskraft'.*
[2] *Gespräch mit Kantler,* F. V. Müller, 29th April 1818.

THE HEART OF A PICTURE

So art turns from reproduction to production—an art of expression. In a little poem which accompanied a portfolio of drawings sent to Merck, Goethe wrote:

> 'Erkenne jedes Dings Gestalt,
> Sein Leid und Freud, Ruh und Gewalt,
> Und fühle, wie die ganze Welt
> Der grosse Himmel zusammenhält:
> Dann du ein Zeichner, Kolorist,
> Haltungs-und Ausdrucksmeister bist.'[1]
>
> (Sophienausgabe, I Abt., 4 Bd., p. 195)

"Haltungs-und Ausdrucksmeister!" Master of the characteristic expression. Surprising words, but they show that Goethe, like Klee, had experienced what Klee described as 'an intensified vision of an object' or 'a humanization of an object'. Goethe goes on to say that seeing produces 'a constant, living bond between the eye of the spirit and the eyes of the body'.[2] The external world is 'the response or reflection which corresponds to individual feelings',[3] because 'the appearance is not freed from the spectator, but is on the contrary involved with and consumed by the individuality of the spectator'. Goethe attempted in his *Allgemeine Glaubens·Bekenntnis*[4] of 1815 to reduce his experiences to a formula:

(a) In nature there is everything that is in the individual.
(Y) And something more.
(b) In the individual there is everything that is in nature.

---

[1] The following is an approximate translation: 'Recognize the form of everything, its pain and joy, peace and might, and feel how the heavens hold the whole world together. Then you will be a draughtsman, colourist and master of the characteristic expression.'

[2] *Paralipomena zur Farbenlehre.*

[3] Ibid.

[4] General Statement of Beliefs.

(Z) and something more.

(b) can recognize (a), (Z) can only guess at (Y).

(a) can be experienced through observation, (Y) cannot.

But (Y) can be made apprehensible through some activity.[1]

Hence the postulate: 'There is an unknown but law-abiding quantity in every object which corresponds to some unknown but law-abiding quantity in the individual.' The world within and the world without form a whole, and that is what Klee tried to explain by means of the drawing reproduced in the Chapter '*Ways of Studying Nature*'. There is perhaps no more apposite comment on this than a sentence which occurs in Goethe's *Farbenlehre*: 'The eye reflects the world without and the man within. The total unity of the without and the within is completed by the eye.'[2]

Another important point: Y = the unknown but law-abiding quantity in an object which can be made apprehensible through some activity because it corresponds to an unknown but law-abiding quantity in the individual. The individual originates the activity, which is productive. Therefore Goethe regarded genius as being synonymous with 'productive power' or the 'formative nature in man'. And understanding of the world is to be found 'in man's productive response to the world, which involves the totality of human nature'. Goethe, like Klee, knew that action, thought-action, releases in us things previously unknown, which suddenly burst upon our consciousness and for that reason often seem like heaven-sent inspirations. Goethe says: 'On a higher plane one can not know but one must act, just as when playing a game there is little to know and everything to do.'

[1] To C. H. Schlosser, 19th February 1815.
[2] *Paralipomena zur Farbenlehre*, Sophienausgabe, Naturw. Schriften, 5, p. 12.

THE HEART OF A PICTURE

Let us now apply this to the realm of picture-making and ask ourselves where it is that things happen. Klee the painter answers: in the orientation on the formal plane, in the activity of classifying and arranging, in the realm of organization of the pictorial means, where it is decided whether, and if so what sort of, a picture will be born. Goethe was not, except in a minor degree, a pictorial artist, yet whenever he turned to art he adopted the same principle. His orientation on the formal plane appears in his *Farbenlehre*, for although this was, admittedly, a scientific work it was nevertheless conceived as a communication from one artist to others. Nothing accidental is admitted, and Goethe is at pains to discover laws of creation, compulsions in Nature, which can be applied creatively when working with the element of colour. Goethe's science is not 'disinterested', for his object is to describe 'the law-abiding quality of nature in relation to the function of the eye'.[1] That indeed is 'science applied to action', or according to Goethe's definition—art.

Goethe's reflections on how to master the formal means were bound to be incomplete, for he was not primarily a pictorial artist. He concentrated on another medium: language. Artistic activity was of course also involved there, and on that account Goethe, like Klee, knew that during the process of sorting and arranging unconscious forces inside us are brought into play. For 'man cannot tarry long in a state of consciousness; he must retire again into the unconscious, for that is where his roots are'. This then is the store-chamber, as we have called it, where something complete and typical is born out of all our submerged experiences, adventures, thoughts, memories and dreams. From there it enters our consciousness and is recognized, or else it appears as a picture before our

---

[1] *Farbenlehre*, Didaktischer Teil, p. xxii.

159

eyes. 'All that we discover or, on a higher plane, uncover is the result of making significant use of an original feeling for truth which, having been silently cultivated for a long while, suddenly and with amazing rapidity leads to the recognition of something fruitful.'[1]

Enough has been said to prove that Klee's use of the word 'Romanticism' was justified, for he is in the line of Classical-Romantic thought. That is a spiritual confession which enables us to follow this line of thought on from Carl Gustav Carus, down to the present day, where it has acquired a new vitality. Whilst Klee was thinking about the origins of form, about the creation of form, and about how the cosmos is reflected in man, biological thought began to move in the same direction. Goethe's ideas on morphology caused very little stir in his own time and were soon swept away by the positivist beliefs of nineteenth century science. But in our own century they have suddenly become actual again owing to a completely different scientific approach, and the study of form plays a tremendous part to-day in all branches of biology.[2] Were this the appropriate place, I would attempt to demonstrate that contemporary thought is already caught up in the characteristic spiral in which ideas develop and will soon have returned to a position abandoned more than a hundred years ago, but on another plane. Romanticism has now entered its acute phase, for to-day artists have the means to carry out ideas and types of composition which were only dreamt of by romantics of an earlier generation. This is largely due to the insight into the independent significance of coloured forms won after a struggle by certain modern painters who regarded painting as a

---

[1] *Maximen und Reflexionen*, Ed. Hecker, No. 562.
[2] *vide* W. Troll, *Gestalt und Urbild, Grundgedanken der organischen Morphologie.* (Halle, 1942).

REVOLT OF THE VIADUCT, 1937
Kunsthalle, Hamburg

NORTH ROOM, 1932
Klee Gesellschaft, Bern

means of making man's world of expression visible. Paul Klee was one of these, and he set out to achieve something proclaimed by Goethe in his '*Maxims*': 'Seek within yourself. There you will find everything. And you should rejoice if, outside of yourself, or whatever you like to call it, you find something in Nature which says "Yes" and "Amen" to everything that you find in yourself. We know of no world except in relation to man; we want no art which is not a likeness of this relationship.'[1]

However, spiritual considerations such as these are secondary so far as we are concerned. All that was intended was to try and give the fullest meaning to the word 'imago', the root-word from which comes 'imagination', which covers all that we have been discussing. And perhaps, by invoking the support of such a brilliant intellect as Goethe, its meaning has been conveyed. 'Imago'—there we have the likeness of the relationship between man and his world. Thus having gained a profound insight into the genesis of form and Nature's superior organizing powers, our spiritual power of intuitive judgment is able to pick out what is typical, what can be given form. This then becomes the raw material from which many images are fashioned. We absorb things through our eyes, they then pass into our innermost self, become an integral part of our vital impulses, and provide, in our unconscious, the raw material from which our ever active, formative imagination fashions pictures. Stimulated by our half-meditative, half-playful artistic activity, it then passes from the unconscious on to the canvas at the moment of creation, as a picture which is entirely our own, and which has entered our eye from within. So the indissoluble unity of the world within and the world without is completed in the eye. Thus the

---

[1] *Maximen und Reflexionen*, No. 1077, to Schadow.

imago ends as a working formula for the imagination, and this imago is the heart of the picture.

Is this true of Klee? Is it true of our picture? I believe that it is, and that only now do we know what this picture is, because only now can we unravel the story of its birth. The sequence of events must have been as follows. At the age of fifty, Klee at last realized one of his life's ambitions, and went to Egypt. Conscious of historical associations, he looked around him and accumulated visual knowledge. He saw the fruitful, alluvial soil of the Nile valley being alternately flooded and dried and bearing traces of having being tilled for thousands of years by the fellaheen. The picture was constantly changing, yet each of its hundred forms was but a variation of a single picture— the typical pictorial configuration underlying them all. And as he looked, Klee saw the higher type of organized relation-ship underlying the complexity of individual appearances in the landscape. That sank into him, sank into his unconscious, where pictorial memories cannot be distinguished from crea-tions of our own fantasy, where they 'become our life-blood, both gesture and expression, nameless', as Rilke says. The scene now changes to the artist's studio. It is the moment of creation and Klee is trying, with the help of the artistic means, to discipline an abstract web of rhythmic, amorphous lines and changing forms which have found their way instinctively on to his canvas. He had nothing in mind that he was trying to represent when, all of a sudden, there emerged this long-meditated image. This was a dream of his own, an image which corresponded to his spiritual state. It was entirely abstract, since he had never seen it, and yet the whole forma-tion of the Egyptian landscape is summed up in this pictorial type-sign. For now we can see that, although it is neither a naturalistic nor a photographic reproduction of something

THE HEART OF A PICTURE

seen, this picture has its own intensity and is a record of the experiences, thoughts and dreams which were liberated in the artist when he looked at ancient Egypt changed into form. It is as though Egypt were seen from an immense, abstract distance, and the whole picture is full of a mythical harmony. It is a communication which has been given form, an ideogram; and like the ideograms of earlier centuries it is a frozen, hieratic image of the constantly changing face of Nature and the activities of man. Transfixed in an imago. This imago is the heart of the picture.

Would the picture then originate in a memory? Only relatively speaking, only if by memory we mean something as deep as the Greek '*mnemosyne*', the mother of the Muses. Or in the Platonic sense, when all knowledge gained is represented as a series of memories, as something 'discovered within oneself'. Or in the sense of a memory which can stretch from the remotest realms of mythology to the 'dead and the still unborn', to quote a phrase of Klee's. Nevertheless we too know something of the myth-forming power of memory, for we often talk about memory lending colour to things and experiences. Memory enhances our view of things through its power to make them unreal. But it does more. Out of truth and poetry, memory builds something higher, for it raises things and events to the plane of legend. It sees things from a great abstract distance, and so enables us to perceive their universality, their sign-formation, their form. With Klee, every visual experience and its corresponding human emotions passed through the filters of memory. Each filter removed some of the coarseness of reality, so that the raw material was constantly being refined until the visual experience took precise form as a clear pictorial idea and its corresponding emotions were infused with a poetic nostalgia. Thus a picture by Klee achieved what seemed impossible, for it was an image of something actually existing as mirrored in the myth-making vision of man.

Memory? Our knowledge about its formative powers is a comparatively recent discovery. Marcel Proust, who looked for inspiration in his awareness of the retentive powers of memory, was one of the first to point the way. Henri Bergson investigated its powers philosophically. Aby Warburg investigated the effect of the myth-making powers of memory on the interpretation of history. Thus it was not until the present century that we became conscious of the formative power of memory. Such then is the perspective in which we must see Paul Klee.

But this word 'memory' must not be given too much prominence for there is a danger of it acquiring too much of an objective meaning. The fact that an imago is the heart of a picture carries us beyond objective representation into another dimension. It also signifies something inactive in man; indeed, it is a complex pictorial sign for this. For the imago is a likeness of the relationship between the world and man, and at that point the expressions 'representational' and 'abstract' lose their descriptive values. In any case a picture by Klee must be experienced as something abstract, for on this depends our ability to interpret it. And if we read something representational into it, then it is by virtue of the evocative power of the signs which he has evolved out of his abstract formal structure. The handling of form is the basis of picture-making.

Chapter X

THE HANDLING OF FORM

It is not easy to set out Klee's pictorial achievements in chronological order. He had such complete command over the whole range of the pictorial means that he could have done anything at any time. Some problems occupied him throughout the whole of his life, for instance how to combine an abstract background pattern of colour with a superimposed but subsidiary drawing; this he first attempted in 1910. His perpetual curiosity kept him spiritually alert to any little stimulus from the world around him. Even a student's mistakes, or a teacher's doodles, could excite and stimulate him to some new experiment. For Klee's productive power was an essential part of his personality and was the means by which it was liberated. And individual pictures—each perfect in itself —were but by-products of a constant straining towards higher spiritual things. 'Klee the man dominated Klee the artist', Walter Gropius has said. His first pupil who worked with him in Bern in 1904, like his colleagues at the Bauhaus, all agree that there was no appeal from Klee's judgment. He regarded art as a means of expressing a moral attitude, of realizing ever-growing spiritual aspirations, but he also regarded it as an experimental field by which both elements were affected. So Klee was always receptive to anything and was not in the least concerned about the chronology of his work. He did not set out to paint a biography of himself and so he quite often produced replicas of earlier works. He would pick up something that he had done many years before and feel that he had to do it again in a different size or a different medium. Thus in 1935 he painted a large second version (1·50×100 cm.) of a small tempera painting of 1932 entitled '*Hat, Lady and Little Table*', in which the little idyll acquired a dangerous intensity. This second version was entitled '*Dame Demon*'. On another occasion, in 1934, he took a large drawing of 1930 called '*The Creator*' and turned it into an oil painting; both these works however are executed in an idiom like plaiting composed of parallel strips, which he frequently used in 1926–7. But in spite of stylistic traits which reoccur over long periods of time, and in spite of the variety of formal solutions, it is not difficult to date Klee's pictures once one has understood certain fundamental characteristics in the development of their formative procedure. Klee's conception of form developed through the years and this can be described in broad outline.

We have already remarked that during the years 1920–1. when Klee first went to the Bauhaus, his work showed a slight but decided leaning towards constructivism. The structure of a picture such as '*Autumnal Place*' had a new tension and firmness which made everything he had done earlier look a bit illustrative, or fairy-tale like, as though they were pages out of a 'cosmic picture book', to quote a familiar phrase. This fairy-tale world appears as in a peep-show on the little stage of which puppets, surprised by their own accomplishments, are acting out charming fables. A '*Weltbeukunst*' of high romance! The construction of the picture is perfectly balanced, but it seems like something cut out from a fantastic world, something which one might perhaps see on another world or another planet. It is a world put together with elements taken from this world and from the cosmos, from reality and from the dream-world, from abstractions and from material things. But in the second reality of the picture they appear real and can be represented in a kind of 'realistic' excerpt. This is true even of such masterly paintings as '*Full Moon*' or '*The Cock and the Grenadier*', both of which were painted under the influence of Braque and the Cubists. Compared with the works of modern French painters, Klee's pictures have something illustrative about them, also a descriptive colourfulness which owes something to the naïve element in folk art and children's art.

In 1921 Klee's pictures became more crystalline. He began to form mosaic-like compositions with small geometrical forms, irregular quadrilaterals and simplified natural forms, binding the individual formal elements together in a proportional relationship which seems to be based on the science of numbers. This crystalline growth extends across the entire picture. A fine web of lines runs from left to right and from top to bottom; this is the veiled framework into whose superior organization the forms fit in a pre-determined order. We are immediately reminded of weaving, where the network of warp and weft provides the structure within which forms can move. Or else we are reminded of stained glass, where the leads provide a kind of lattice structure. Then we remember that Klee was summoned to the Bauhaus to take over the teaching of weaving and glass-painting. Now it is not irrelevant to consider what, if anything, Klee found to borrow from the technique of these crafts to help him with picture-making. Something was of course borrowed, and this is confirmed by the fact that it was in 1921 that Klee first attempted perspectival pictures. These are pictures of interiors, seen in strict centralised perspective, which are imposed upon an abstract coloured background, and they were undoubtedly inspired by the novel forms of perspectival drawings produced by the architects at the Bauhaus. For the next few years Klee continued to interest himself in these perspectives of cube-like rooms, which have a sort of eerie charm just because they are executed with such exactness.

Yet Klee's interest in and experiments with the novel technical means which he discovered at the Bauhaus had very little effect on his attempt to make his pictures firmer and more self-sufficient. This tendency in his work was a reaction against the formal chaos of Expressionism, and that accounts for his cautious but unmistakable acceptance of the ideas of the Constructivists and of Piet Mondrian, all of whom were highly esteemed at the Bauhaus. We must not forget, however, that as early as 1903 Klee had recognized that 'picture-making never starts from a poetic mood or idea, but with the construction of one or more figures, with the harmonizing of certain colour and tone values, or with the setting aside of spatial relationships, etc'. Now at last he was able to put this belief into practice and he began to conceive of a picture as an independent organism which had to be complete within the rectangle of its frame. Klee dispensed with an illusion of space, using instead flat planes piled one on top of the other and interlocking as though the picture were clasping its hands. This at once brings to mind what Cézanne said to Gasquet. 'Are you pleased to-day?' said Gasquet. 'I've got hold of my *motif*', replied Cézanne, clasping his hands together so that the fingers interlocked. 'There, that's what a *motif* is like', and unclasping and reclasping his hands in order to demonstrate something to Gasquet he went on: 'That's what one has to obtain. Not one link must be too weak, there must not be a hole anywhere through which emotion, light or truth can slip. I work on every part of my canvas simultaneously, so that I catch and bring together in a single action anything that is trying to slip away. Everything we see gets dispersed, disappears. . . . So that is why I clasp my two errant hands together. I take things

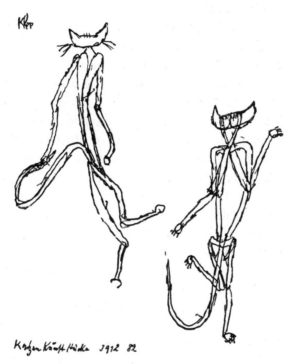

Cat Acrobats, 1912, *Private Collection*

from left and right, from here and there, everywhere, tonalities, colours, nuances. I fix them and bring them together. They become lines, objects, rocks, trees, without my thinking about it. They acquire volume and value. And if these volumes and values correspond on my canvas, in my sensibility, to the planes and patches of colour that I have before my eyes, well then my picture clasps its hands! It does not vacillate. It is neither above nor below the mark. It is true, it is dense, it is replete.' Already in 1910, when Klee first saw pictures by Cézanne, he recognized that this was the master *par excellence*. He too had finally succeeded in making his pictures clasp their hands.

As this new development followed its course after 1922, Klee's poetic discoveries were expressed in ever larger, simpler forms. There is a bold drawing of '*Ptarmigans*' in which the birds are set between stiff, leafy plants, and icy air. A bell-shaped flower emits '*Silver-Moon Chimes*'. In this picture a small scroll-like flower has been greatly enlarged, a covering like a belfry has been built round its peal of chimes and the cool, silvery light of the moon pours through its rafters. The small, bell-shaped flower is enclosed in a heavy architectural construction. In '*Fire Wind*' tongues of flame, like great futurist scrolls, are being blown through the windows of a building and are scorching its bare walls as they pass.

Klee also applied his constructive handling of the pictorial means to his handling of colour. In a picture called '*Growth of Nocturnal Plants*', a series of extravagant forms like plants, lit by a pale light, are growing in front of a midnight background. The compelling impression of growth is due to a rhythmic piling-up of formal units: first a kidney-shaped form, then a circular one, then an angular one. The growth of each plant conforms to this same triple rhythm, though some are taller than others. This growth-rhythm also affects the handling of colour. The base of each plant is a neutral grey which develops to a cold blue in its third unit; it then passes via a neutral light grey to warm orange in its sixth unit; and again it passes via grey to a cold whitish blue in its ninth unit, where it cools off. Thus a fully developed plant consists of a triple rhythm re-

170

GROWTH OF NOCTURNAL PLANTS, 1922

Stangl Gallery, Munich

peated three times, the same rhythm being repeated in the handling of the colour, which runs from neutral to cold, from cold to warm and back again to cold. Thus the simple rhythmic growth of form, which is reinforced by the rhythmic changes of colour (from cold to warm and back to cold), is enough to suggest to us the growth of a plant. Poetry develops out of the deliberate disciplining of the pictorial means, and thus the picture becomes a simile for Nature.

This system was however capable of development, and so, in 1923, Klee started to build pictorial structures with coloured cubes. And as he placed the bricks of colour side by side, he found that their differences in size and colour drew them together and set up an autonomous rhythm. At first they had no objective signification. But sometimes the building-up process would suggest to him some architectural association, and then the picture would take objective form as 'Castles', 'Towers' or 'Architecture'. Pictorially speaking, however, nothing more was involved than a rhythmic ordering of coloured forms. Mondrian hovers in the background and his colleagues at the Bauhaus regarded the chessboard as the highest structural organization of a surface. This was a problem that Klee never dropped, indeed he came back to it time and again. In 1927 he produced some '*Constructive-impressive*' oriental buildings with columns; in 1930 he painted some pictures with rhythmic rows of black and white, for example '*Three-time in the Rectangle*'; then in 1937 he produced the large '*Superchess*' belonging to the Zurich Kunsthaus; and in 1940 '*Glass Façade*'.

This new procedure had a considerable effect in enriching and making more systematic his use of colour in water-colours. By 1923 already Klee was allowing his water-colours to develop constructively. He drew horizontal lines in rich, clear colours across the whole surface, then filled these in with strips of colour washed on perpendicularly. Thus he obtained a coloured scaffolding which served as a structural framework. The surface was covered with a network, and the role of colour was to create a sense of space through the differences in depth between the various tones. Klee applied colour in transparent overlapping washes, suggesting planes, and at the same time began methodically to investigate how its effects were obtained and to emphasize its magic. The magic of colour. Yes, for out of the association-values of the rich, transparent, glowing colours and the structure of rectangular surfaces, wondrous and remote images appeared, seen as though through a stained glass window—walls, towers, cathedrals, reflections. Then the scaffolding lying across the surface of the picture also took on a magic significance. It forced the picture back into some remote, abstract realm and acted like a fence through which one could peer into mysterious rooms on some intangible, enchanted world. Windows into something remote, a magic lantern. Delaunay too knew something about this sort of magic, and in 1914 Macke also had tried to make use of it.

Remote and often mythical pictures can be glimpsed through the fence, for example a picture such as '*The Mount of the Bull*'. Here the scaffolding spreads diagonally across the surface of the picture. From a light, clear ochre at the centre, the colours get dimmer as they move outwards towards the edges through increasingly thick washes of dark brown. There remains a light-coloured pyramid which suggests something oriental, something to do with fanatical ancient cults. Klee gladly took the hint. He put the sheet on which he had produced this abstract structure underneath another sheet, covered with black printer's ink, through which he drew as his fantasy dictated. He often resorted to this technique in water-

172

colours when he wanted to combine a drawing with a coloured background, for the indirectness of the procedure made it easier for him to spin his little fairy tales. In the picture under discussion, Klee set up a steep flight of steps leading to the area of most light, in which he placed a statue of a bull. Dancing in the half-light at its base is a terrified priestly figure, a sort of Tibetan magician, gesticulating as though hypnotized. Like a marionette whose strings are held by the idol, he comes skipping up the flight of steps. Now it was the 'fence' which made it possible for Klee to look into the remote depths and bring up this image from the realm of fairy tale and mythology. But we ourselves can experience something of the same sort by looking at stained glass windows in a church; for the bits of brightly coloured glass set in a black framework of lead are apt to suggest something mysterious which we cannot properly identify.

Now apart from those pictures of Klee in which an air of mystery is achieved through the colour-construction, there are others of the same period in which the colour-magic is handled in a different though related way. They too have an exotic charm reminiscent of the magic images of the Incas or of some oriental people. The formal structure of these pictures is created by a black silhouette like a stencil being placed on top of a brightly coloured ground. This produces combinations of secret signs behind which there is an enigmatic glow, so that these pictures look like something primeval, demonic and mythical which might have come from a wall decoration in a buried city. This was just the sort of atmosphere which Klee loved to create. These pictures are flat, their tonality is dark, and the various demonic signs sit like incrustations on the surface beneath which flickers a fire of colour.

The controlled romanticism of the style permits the artist a wide range of expression which embraces at one end severe mathematical constructions and at the other a rich vein of myth and poetry. Klee composes, builds, weighs and arranges with the intelligence of a master-builder. Yet his pictures do not lose their spiritual quality because, by an ingenious use of the pictorial means, he can relegate objects and living things to a remote and legendary realm, to that realm 'which used to be symbolized by the halo of sainthood', to quote Van Gogh. In 1924–5, in an effort to test the range of expression at his command, Klee made short trips to the Baltic seaboard and to Sicily. These experiences were recorded in a series of dream-like, half-remembered images, for example in a picture of sand dunes by moonlight. Everything seemed remote and ghostly, in this light, and the tall prickly things growing out of the sand look like goblins moving along the edge of a soft purple sea. Here too a sort of magic veil has been thrown over nature, as it disperses, and when we look through this veil we can see in the far distance, in an abstract dimension, an apparition of sand dunes in moonlight. Other pictures are of busy Sicilian harbours, or of aloes and other plants or trees growing beside the Mediterranean. Here colour played the essential part: light tones running from purple to yellow for example, clean and delicately balanced without the harsh notes of their complementaries. Klee wanted to give an idea of something he had seen and enjoyed, an exact impression. But while he was trying to render exactly the source of his enjoyment he discovered certain colour relationships behind his visual experience. So he ended in abstraction for the sake of the visual sensation.

But there was another side to the medal. Sometimes as Klee worked, his construction would take matters into its own hands and he would find himself involved in solving complicated problems of balance between a group of abstract coloured forms, with the see-saw tipping now this way and now that. The picture *'Exercitium in Blue and Orange'* is a good example, for it is based on the greatest span of the chromatic circle. Such pictures involved balancing feats of pure form, for there was no question of pinning down an impression with the magic of colour, nor of helping something unknown to materialize. They were pure musical acrobatics. Against a background of firmly constructed planes, some little matchlike forms indulge in a staccato dance while balancing light-coloured balls on their tips. It is a sort of Japanese conjuring act. Thus pure abstraction is involved but the rigid formulas are concealed beneath charming images which have a life of their own. Yet Klee never fails to capture something poetic, and this is induced by his constructive procedure in the way we have described when talking about the picture *'Moonrise'*.

It would be true to say that the dancing rhythm of this picture is trying to assert itself. One feels that the solid structure of the picture should be set in motion so that the movement of individual forms would merge into the greater movement of the whole. Klee intended this, for in the next year, 1926, he invented a new type of form which changed everything. Klee was always fascinated by the rhythmic impulses which are apparent in writing, and this was the source of his new invention, which was a highly personal style of composition using repetitions of a given motif and rhythm. Parallel configurations were spread across the surface of the picture as if it were woven, thus creating a rich rhythmic pattern (like knots in weaving or embroidery on lace) on top of something plain. Single lines were repeated and thus endowed with great rhythmic force. Klee allowed his psychographic monologue to develop into a rhythmic polyphony swinging in strict tempo across the entire canvas, and at the same time creating a well-defined sense of space. Perhaps it was at this time that Klee became acquainted with the decorative *motifs* of Viking 'plaiting ornament'; at any rate the style of his drawing suggests this. He now drew with parallel strokes small bands which wind in and out of each other, and at the points where they meet they cut a surprising flight of steps into space. Plaiting of this sort produces wonderful images—'*Rayleaf Plants*' or '*Classical Gardens*' for example—and enables him to build flights of steps, or monoliths or sharply receding perspectives —as in the townscape '*Adrastea Polis*'. At the same time, the linear rhythm enables Klee to take daring leaps because the balletic structure of the picture is solid. So he was encouraged to attempt balletic subjects: one such is called '*Being Young*', another is '*In the Temple of Flora*'.

This new approach to form can be explained by a change in Klee's artistic aims, on the formal as well as on the human plane. By 'formal' I mean here the discipline he imposed in building the rhythmic element into the very texture of a picture. The static mathematical element in the construction had to start vibrating. It had to breathe, to move, to lose its rigidity by falling in with the rhythm of the whole: it had to attain the space-time dimension. At the same time Klee had to persuade the pictorial world for which he was searching in the depths of his memory and imagination to yield up its golden secrets at the behest of a rhythmic stimulus. And this brings us to the 'human' plane. Here Klee resorted to the procedure of formal meditation—the turning of the prayer-wheel, the dance of the dervish, the continually repeated call to prayer, the conjuring-up of otherwise unobtainable images. Klee treated his medium as an aid to prayer and induced a state of receptivity in himself with dots and dashes, the con-

FIGURE IN A GARDEN, 1937
Klee Foundation

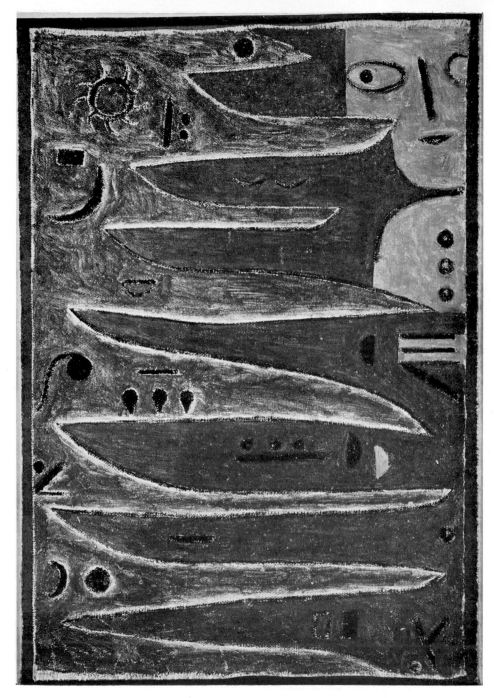

GREYBEARD AND THE COASTLINE, 1938
Klee Foundation

stant repetition of a rhythm and the repeated pattern of interwoven strands. And only when his rhythmic meditation reached its greatest intensity would he hit upon the fundamental image which was crying out to be set free. The more trouble it gave him, the better; the deeper the preparatory work went, the nearer he was to discovery.

In this respect Klee was like a ritual dancer, like another pious Jongleur de Notre-Dame. And the picture that emerged was a transcript of this trance-like, choreographic activity. At the end of this series of formal experiments we have 'Fool in a Trance' painted in 1929, which is also a highly expressive dance subject and must be read as such. For gesture and mime are not the only components of a dance. Leaps and bounds too form part of its expressive repertoire and give shape and human significance to an undefined area of space. In a picture such as 'Fool in a Trance', the record of the dancer's arabesques is linear and consists of an unbroken line darting hither and thither at the dictates of its own rhythm, discovering itself as it progresses. An expressionistic dancer on skates might cut arabesques like these on the ice and so 'experience' the rhythmic movements of his body as an expressive line. For if one follows this line one can 'experience' the interruptions and jerks, inter-sections and lunatic impulses which have produced its movement. The figurative simile arises of its own accord out of this abstract pattern of lines; a figure presents itself and the picture is called 'Fool in a Trance'. An abstract experience has become figuratively concrete, and this in turn has provided the artist with a description for something already implicit in the psychography of his line.

The pictorial structure was first given a rhythm on the graphic plane; this then spread to the picture itself, though at first, because of the nature of the graphic means, the picture consisted of several small entities. Klee tried to overcome this by two methods. Either he gave his picture a monumental appearance by allowing the planes to remain bare and the forms to grow larger. Or he tried to suppress the graphic element and to transfer the rhythmic element into the purer, more controllable realm of colour. The first method meant that he had to renounce what we have called his 'formal meditation'; the second therefore appeared more satisfactory, although obviously fraught with difficulties. Once again, a great visual experience such as he had known long ago in Tunisia put Klee on the right path. This experience was Egypt, for it was there that he saw how to solve the problem of unifying structure, rhythm and colour pictorially. And he owed this discovery to his emotional experience of the formal structure of the landscape of Egypt with its accumulation of broad, horizontal bands which pile upwards and backwards in depth and are traversed by a fine rhythmic network of fields and paths. Klee's 'striped' pictures of 1929 are based on memories of this experience. We have already dealt with '*High way and Byways*'; others of the series are called '*Evening in Egypt*', '*Evening Fire*', '*Monument in the Land of Plenty*', '*Sun-Stripes on the Plain*'. In these the whole picture is composed of horizontal strips of colour laid parallel to each other, narrow ones, wide ones, short ones, long ones; and the lines marking their ends build up a vertical scaffolding which carries the picture upwards. This idea of using parallel bands first appeared as a graphic procedure in 1926, but now it was systematically elaborated, became a constructive pictorial framework, was transposed into the realm of colour and used there in its purest form. Now although this new type of pictorial structure resulted from Klee's experience of the formal structure of the Egyptian landscape, and was in a sense a formal reflection of its grandeur, we must not conceal from ourselves the fact that it was also a pure, independent and abstract formal procedure which derived logically from his ideas of 1923 (building with cubes) and 1926 (rhythmic plaiting). This method of handling form was a successful fusion of the three separate methods used by Klee hitherto. The stripes insure a simple monumental construction covering the whole surface of the picture. Rhythm enters into this striped construction as a movement which sets the whole framework quivering. The keyboard of stripes is then used to beat out a simple but forceful rhythm, which is based, as in music, on certain numerical intervals. And the vertical lines marking the ends of each coloured stripe build up into geometric configurations which give the picture a rhythmic upward growth. But the whole thing, both structure and rhythm, exist entirely in and through colour, because the outline of the scaffolding is created only by the piling-up of small areas of colour. Thus Klee achieved not only the unity he was after but also his second requirement—meditation induced by a formal procedure. As Klee piled one area of colour upon another and allowed an image to develop out of his repeated rhythms, he listened to or felt the pulse-beat of what was growing and acted accordingly. His own psyche began to vibrate, then its wave-length coincided with that of the picture, and ultimately in a flash of recognition Klee was able to give his picture a human and objective significance. At once it ceased to be an abstract construction, ceased to be merely Egypt and became what Delaunay referred to as 'a heart-beat of the artist himself'.

Klee's rhythmic procedure with coloured stripes enabled him to create a strong pictorial structure. Air and space were enclosed within the geometry of the coloured surfaces. But Klee did not want to lose touch with the realm of air, where

179

things hover and move without reference to the earth. He always wanted to range over as wide a field as possible. Structure, rhythm, colour—by the same fusion of these three elements he had to provide a means of bringing this other world to life. His first experiments with it date from 1929. It seems paradoxical perhaps to construct the realm of air, but by now Klee understood the infinite power of the constructive means. So he started applying them to space. The pattern of striped surfaces was turned round ninety degrees; then they pointed into space and suggested an arrangement of spatial planes. The coloured scaffolding created the illusion of receding layers. When Klee first turned his attention to problems of tonality he divided the individual tone-values into spatial planes, then arranged these by piling one on top of the other, and allowed them to develop cumulatively into a scale of black-and-white values. Next he applied this procedure in the realm of colour. Starting from the background, he proceeded to place one coloured form on top of another like a series of transparencies. Each of these forms has a single tonality except where it overlaps another one and there the colour changes to a blend of the two. It is as though each form were cut out in a transparent sheet of colour and several sheets placed on top of each other. By this means a magic, light, transparent effect of space is produced; it is the realm of air, gently mobile and yet constructed, a realm in which individual forms have the power to hover. A flight of steps into the realm of air. The magic of the pictorial means lured Klee on to try and capture the more mobile element of atmosphere. So he drew '*Spirits of the Air*', flat little forms blown by the wind and fluttering like storm-birds. He had found that his transparencies could be given an expressive outline full of movement because the formal procedure was anchored in the realm of space. The outline was

LAND WITCHES, 1938
Klee Foundation

FLOWER, 1938
Collection Hilla Rebay

entirely free; it was the means of expressing the playful tricks of air. 'Scene from an Aerial Hunt' is the title of a picture in which flat transparent little forms, figuratively most expressive, are chased across the surface by arrows of direction—light, spirit-like, flying. Then there are the atmospheric pictures. One is called 'Storm', and another 'Mixed Weather'; these too are characterized by little forms which can be read figuratively as a windswept tree or a scudding cloud. There is also 'Before the Snow'. Here a number of transparent layers of colour slowly advance one by one, out of a background pregnant with darkness; they wrap themselves around a tree, which thus gets a foretaste of the bad weather to come. The transparency of these layers of colour suggested to Klee another transparent element: water. So he created visions of submarine gloom and activity, introducing a few plant symbols on various planes. For example, 'Oceanic Landscape'.

This world of transparencies in which everything hovers or flies was built upon the strict handling of form which we have already described as 'constructing the realm of air'. This procedure alone determines that the result will be an independent formal entity called a 'picture' and not an illustration. The rhythmic procedure is used to create depth, while the layers of receding planes create a colour-space dimension which helps the picture to grow towards its content. In this rhythmic colour-space, which is the true reality of the picture, line is free to wander, the surface can be made to vibrate by means of repetitions, and the construction can acquire a cubic, three-dimensional significance without the picture in any way losing its lightness or having its wings clipped.

As a next step Klee began to expose the cubic scaffolding of the picture and keep it hovering. He hoped that by kicking aside all props he would be left with larger forms and a more monumental effect. For Klee thought of art as a refining process enabling him to go from complicated to simple things, so that the purest form would always end up as its simplest visual equivalent. He felt that the more an artist had to say, the fewer his means should be.

Klee began to attack this problem in 1930, and the pictures he produced were greatly simplified compositions with large forms. But they were bigger in size than before because the forms demanded more room in which to develop. There is juggling with planes, and the role previously played by planes is taken over by simple, geometrical colour formations, mostly rectangles, which are laid out across the surface in a free rhythm. They establish distances and create a colour-space dimension with a crystalline formation of its own which exists in front of the actual background of the picture. Coloured lines anchor each separate rectangle of colour to its position in space. Thus a formation made up of boxes, as it were, comes into being, a strong, rhythmic, cubic formation. This type of formation soon developed an unearthly lightness, a power to take wing which it acquired through being set in the independent colour-space dimension; for this is the second unearthly reality of the picture and everything in it is similarly affected. These firmly built cubes sway gently in the imaginary picture-space, sailing and swimming with remarkable agility through the coloured atmosphere of the picture. '*Hovering*' is the title of one such picture, '*A Town Sailing*' that of another. Then there is '*Rising and Gliding*', one of the last of the series painted in 1932. The handling of form is clear; the many small elements which made up the colour-space dimension in the transparency pictures have been reduced to a minimum; the solid basis of the construction is exposed; and the cubic element has been restored by means of the spatial rhythm. The pure formula has been found for the 'construction of the realm of air'.

This period of intensive work ended unhappily for Klee. In 1928 Gropius resigned from his post as Director of the Bauhaus, and was succeeded by Hannes Meyer, who soon began to impose materialistic sociological doctrines on the whole institution. The conception of the architect as a master of form was discarded in favour of the conception of the architect as a technician satisfying the needs of society. According to this conception the character of a building had to be determined by the function it was destined to fulfil, and so its form became a secondary consideration. A bare wall is the most functional type of wall, Meyer would maintain, because it can be given any shape or painted in any colour which will have the desired psychological effect. So pictures were banished from the walls because they were disturbing, impermanent and individualistic. Now the four painters of the Bauhaus—Klee, Feininger, Schlemmer and Kandinsky—had been summoned there to collaborate with a group of architects whose ideas about form they were to apply in the realm of pictorial thinking. But under the new administration there was clearly no place for them. Schlemmer left the Bauhaus almost at once, and in 1930 Klee decided to accept a professorship which was offered to him by the Fine Arts Academy of Düsseldorf.

As the political situation in Germany deteriorated, attacks on modern painting increased. Nevertheless Kaesbach, who was then Director of the Düsseldorf Academy, courageously offered a post to Klee, against whom the attacks were particularly violent, in order to enable him to escape from the disagreeable political atmosphere of Dessau. There was in fact no subject available for Klee to teach, so at first he took over the workshop where the materials and techniques of painting were studied. This was an aspect of art education that Klee was peculiarly fitted to teach for, as we know, he regarded materials and technique as the two major factors in the growth of forms. He gave up lecturing about the theory of painting and instead gathered round him a small group of pupils whose work he supervised and to whom he talked enthusiastically about the various realms of artistic orientation, about form and nature, and about selecting the appropriate artistic means.

During his last few years at the Bauhaus Klee had become more remote and detached, and this affected his attitude to the world around him. We have seen how Klee's art and his handling of form had become increasingly dependent upon a meditative process. The revelation was awaited with clasped hands, almost with prayer, in the Pauline sense of a form of prayer without words but with much wringing of the hands. At Düsseldorf Klee retired still further into his shell. To those

City of the Lagoons, 1927

around him he seemed like a magician, queer and often in-comprehensible. But everyone who approached him was conscious of his deep humanity, his unworldly goodness, and this added to the impression that he was something more than just a normal human being.

About this time Klee's painting was greatly affected by his meditative detachment. He did not, however, for a moment give up trying to solve certain urgent problems, for Klee was essentially a painter and his moral code found expression as a formal ethos. He had to complete the task which had been entrusted to him.

Klee had mastered the formative process so far as colour-space construction and its rhythmical proportions were concerned, and we should perhaps already have drawn attention to the fact that in the realm of air, where things hover, the colour is much lighter. Indeed these pictures are full of light. '*Hovering*' for example consists of a pale green background in

the middle of which is a pale pink form. The geometric spatial structure of box-like forms is painted yellow, light blue and ochre. Other pictures of the same kind are executed in light blue and pink, with hovering constructions painted in yellow, Indian red and light purple. This play of colours releases light, but this light is not represented as an independent element with all that that implies in the way of reflections and vibrations. Klee still had to attempt a development in that direction, that is to say he could try incorporating the separate colour vibrations of light and atmosphere. He had still not faced up to light as an independent element: this was a realm governed by chance.

A picture of 1932, '*North Room*', will suffice to show how Klee posed and solved this problem. The most striking thing about this picture is that Klee has reduced to a minimum the gradations of light between the different colours in order to separate their suggestive light value from their degree of luminosity. The picture is keyed in a coloured grey scale, whose light values extend from blue-grey to yellow-grey. The colour is cool and dull. At first, the formal origins of this picture appear complicated, but they can easily be traced by an analytical eye. The bottom part is painted in large dots of colour, for the most part cold in tone; there is so little contrast here that the rhythm is hardly accentuated. They are broken into by a series of emphatic blue-grey lines which set up a rhythm and determine the form of the construction. These lines serve to bring out the vaguely indicated colour-rhythm and then spread across the coloured background in a network of open and closed rectangles. This network has been superimposed over the coloured background. Now if we could take the background and the scaffolding separately we would find ourselves looking at a rhythmic construction about whose development we could foretell nothing. Indeed without the assistance of the spatial medium the scaffolding might have remained simply something superimposed upon, but without any connection with, the background. Klee however turned light into the unifying element on this occasion and achieved a fusion by means of light-vibrations. Patiently and with deliberation he added dot after dot of colour, covering the range from dark to light blue-grey on the cold scale, from purple through red to an occasional orange on the warm scale. And the effect of using these dots was that neither the colour of the background nor that of the dot itself stands out separately; together however they produce coloured light. Thus a background colour, a linear scaffolding and a pullulation of coloured dots, combined to produce something new and material, something which did not exist before, that is to say a colour-light-space in which all three elements are fused into a continuous spatial effect created by light.

This procedure appears to be closely related to the *pointillisme* of the Neo-Impressionists, and it is natural that such a solid construction should remind us of the way in which Seurat composed a picture. So let us for a moment pursue the comparison. What is the purpose of this picture? The title tells us: '*North Room*'. Klee's meditative procedure with dots of colour led to the discovery of light. The dark scaffolding fitted into the scheme. Areas of light shine out like lamps. The abstract construction suddenly became coherent and, as the artist went on working, an effect of diffused light came into being and the dark lines of the scaffolding took on the shapes of identifiable objects—chairs, tables and lamps. There it was— a chilly room in which areas of warm light are trying to raise the temperature. Here then we have an association of ideas which is indicated by the title '*North Room*'.

Everything that we have deduced about the picture by studying its formal origins is confirmed by the title. This picture is indeed concerned with the representation of light, with the creation of a colour-light-space, and our interpretation of the artist's aims is confirmed by other pictures of the same series. One is called '*Light and Other Things*', another '*Open-air Still-life*'. There are also vibrantly luminous landscapes such as '*Classical Seaboard*', which might almost be called impressionistic. Lastly there are imaginary subjects such as '*Landscape UOL*'.

Impressionist and imaginary? In our eagerness to pursue a historical parallel with *pointillisme* we have already taken a wrong road. Klee is no doubt connected in some mysterious way with Seurat, but this particular series of pictures by Klee has nothing in common with the impressionistic aims of *pointillisme*. Klee's pictures exist in quite another reality, in the alternative, abstract, independent reality of the picture itself. They did not originate as descriptions of things seen; they exist independently of the spatial perspective of nature; and they were not inspired by a given set of visual facts. By a pure use of the pictorial means, the artist has created an immaterial world of light which exists in the picture alone and has nothing to do with nature. This is a second reality which becomes 'natural' through the natural growth of the picture. The surface of the picture opens on to an immaterial world; it is not a window which opens on to nature. Behind the shimmer there is a formative power at work seeking to find an equivalent for light.

An equivalent for light? This existed once before the world became secularized. The gold mosaic backgrounds on the walls of Rome, Ravenna and Venice illuminated, with their shimmering light, windows which looked away from this world towards an unearthly realm. Klee had forgotten about this ex-

PARK NEAR LU, 1938
Klee Foundation

WEEPING WOMAN, 1939
Klee Foundation

perience for some thirty years when suddenly he remembered it. Dot by dot and stone by stone he then began to construct his own window on to the unearthly realm and to gaze through it meditatively. What did he see? Nothing sacred, lost or exhausted. Instead he saw the dreams of men, the far-away things of life, the magic light of man's melancholy when he is quite alone amid the reality of his expressive world, the ceremonial hieroglyphics of '*Mosaic of the City Proun*' which no one can decipher because Proun never existed. Now we can see that the technique of applying colour in dots, a technique which provided Klee with the material out of which to construct his colour-light-space, had a deeper significance. For it is also the material of creation in that it leads on to that other dimension where the prayer-wheel creaks, where the ritual drum beats out the rhythm of the cult, and where hands are wrung in silence. Meditation on form: such was the spiritual exercise of this incomparably pure painter. Dot upon dot: that is the call to prayer. Plane upon plane: that is the ladder by which man descends into himself. And as he meditates in the depths of his self he discovers images which reveal this self to him.

Now let us turn back to our picture. This was not just something to which the artist had to give an objective interpretation, a North Room, an effect of light created by pictorial means and nothing more. Behind it—though the Philistines may not be able to see it—is the wringing of hands, meditation, and a formative procedure which we might almost associate with a far superior Being. Supposing Klee had been able to rely on the spiritual support of other human beings?—'We do not yet possess that last degree of strength, for we are not supported by a people'—Such were the closing words of Klee's lecture 'On Modern Art'.

Alone—Klee certainly attained as much as any single painter can. The formal laws governing the construction of colour-light-space completed the cycle which had begun with a simple use of the graphic means. Klee is in complete command of his realm, but he is alone. So he must take refuge again in dreams, in meditation. Thus as he says he 'often dreams of a work which will encompass a tremendous range, covering the whole range of means, representation, content and style. It will certainly remain a dream, but it is very healthy now and again to play with the idea of some such possibility, even though to-day it is remote'. Klee knows that he can never achieve it because the present state of society does not permit it. Klee has climbed to the topmost pinnacle which man is permitted to reach. He has left us a full record of the pictorial possibilities and of the subject-matter available to an artist of his day, and he has fully demonstrated the limit of growth to which the human race has attained. That is why he seems to be a little bit more than an ordinary human being.

Chapter XI

TOWARDS THE ANGELS

The moment in Klee's life had come when he faced the future alone. In working out his own destiny he had gradually drifted away from those who had been his companions on the journey. The happy days at the Bauhaus were over; gone too were the pleasant daily meetings with Kandinsky, Schlemmer and Feininger, and the cheerful company of his students. There was none of this in Düsseldorf, where Klee's work with the students was more a matter of indicating and advising. No longer was he a 'master of form' working communally with a group of apprentices and building pictorial structures. The hand of fate pointed to a hermit's cell and a life of solitary meditation.

By an appalling paradox, however, it was at this moment that politics altered the course of his life. Germany echoed with loudly proclaimed slogans such as 'The People', 'Honour', 'Greatness' and 'The Community'. But they were proclaimed by a band of power-lusting thugs whose one aim was to overthrow the moral criteria on which their value rested. With iconoclastic fury these creatures smashed or burnt the precious creations of dedicated individuals, filling the void and the deathly silence which they left behind them with the noise of inhuman political slogans. Thus it was that Klee, one of the purest, gentlest and most good-hearted of men, whose whole life had been spent transforming a high moral conception into a formal ethic, was suddenly proclaimed a 'cultural Bolshevist'. Both Klee and Kaesbach were summarily dismissed from the Düsseldorf Academy in 1933, their houses were searched and many documents seized. Thus the one artist whose moral authority was recognized by all true artists in Germany, and by all who knew him, was forced to leave the country. Klee then returned to Bern.

There is however no need to attribute too much of the blame for the destruction of this remarkable man's life to the German people. In a moving obituary tribute to Paul Klee on 5th July 1940, Georg Schmidt uttered these words: 'Paul Klee's whole life, his growth, his development and his end, were governed by the dictates of some profound law.' The spiral of Klee's life led him back to the place from which he had started, but on a higher plane where he was detached and lonely. And friends who knew him during his last years in Bern have described him as 'a gentle, magical apparition floating amid the crowd'. The door had closed behind him and Klee was in his cell. The fateful clamour had served a good purpose, for it had opened the door to the world of silent contemplation.

Nor was this all. Klee had abandoned Germany, but Switzerland was slow to grant him asylum. What was he then? No longer a German, and yet not Swiss. Of course, he was a European. But was that enough? He was a man. And because his communications proceeded from the very core of his human existence, his art had a force which had long sufficed to make it known beyond the frontiers of Europe. During the last few decades we have witnessed the gradual overthrow of regional cultures, but Klee was one of the first who pointed the way

Over and Up, 1931

towards a new world-culture. He was fascinated and stimulated by all forms of cultural activity: the magic of prehistoric paintings, the dream-like enchantment of oriental art, the profound wisdom of the art of the Far East, the fearful imagery of Peru, the demonic art of Mexico, the powerful rhythm of African negro art. And Klee knew about all that without moving from the romantic heart of Europe. So he was a German, a European and everything else at the same time. And if we may be permitted to use a term which is often applied when speaking of Fra Angelico, of Enguerrand Charenton or of Konrad Witz for example, Klee was the 'primitive' of a new sensibility which will enable mankind to reach greater spiritual creations. For the constellation which governed Klee's pictorial discoveries now also governs science, philosophy and sociological doctrines. Klee's life was governed by the dictates of some profound law. When he forsook Germany and was granted asylum in the country where he had spent his childhood, that too, like everything else about his life, was symbolic of the working of this superior law. Everything was cast off and Klee stood on the frontier between the old and the new cycle in the history of man. But these are perspectives of which Klee himself knew nothing. Fate called and its finger pointed the way to solitude, to a cell full of far-off echoes in which he could pursue his unworldly meditations, and where his life was to end. It was from there that he addressed his last communications to us.

Now if I think of Klee's late work I see before my eyes a small sheet of paper. It is not much of a thing, and would be easy to overlook among the pile of large pictures (some as large as six feet,) executed at this time. This is a distinctly small sheet of thin parchment-like paper painted in gouache in dark, earthy colours: grey, dark ochre, black. It

Inside the Body's Cavern, 1940

195

was painted in 1940, the year of Klee's death. Now one must try to imagine this wonderful but progressively ageing man, living for a long while in the shadow of death, but listening to the sands of time running out and carefully observing every manifestation of growth or decay within himself. Bent over his drawing-board, Klee listens, or sits and meditates. It is a dark moment. Then suddenly something within him seeks to communicate itself. So he begins. He tries to catch the distant voice which is calling, the communication of this dark moment, the hieroglyphic which offers itself. He begins to write, and the colour responds nocturnally: the background becomes grey, and a dull glow of fire is apparent in the redness of the ochre. At the bottom, out of which the picture grows, the grey turns to blue and becomes quite cold. As it shivers, the cold grey begins to leap and this turns into a wavy line running across the paper, which gives the dark, swimming mass of colour a heavy gliding effect. Then lines start to appear—black strokes. A curved sign in the top left corner creates a dark constellation: flowing water and a world growing continually darker. The writing continues. The black strokes stalk bravely on through the darkness, then break off. A new form-determining urge takes over and achieves a construction like the keel of a boat. Then another urge intervenes, this time straining upwards; its beat is repeated four times, and then the floating construction, its sails full, starts moving towards the right. The next to appear are those who are making this journey: two figurative signs. One, bending over, holds the tiller; the other, upright in pale grey, who is solemnly supported and pushed forward with a gesture of holy dread by his companion, is the passenger on this voyage to Hades. '*Dark Voyage*' is the title Klee gave to his picture, but to us it suggests Charon's boat. More is implied here than is immediately appa-

DARK VOYAGE, 1940
Klee Gesellschaft, Bern

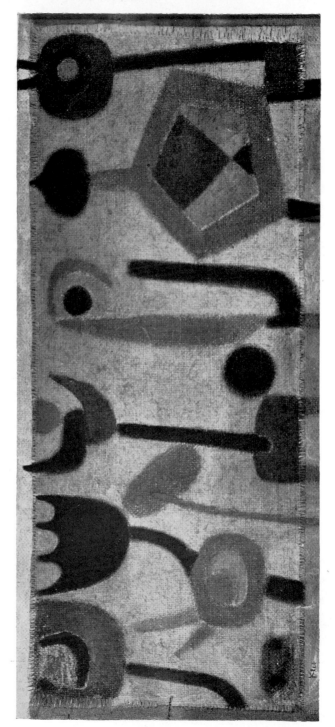

TWILIGHT BLOOMS, 1940
Klee Foundation

rent. The significance of the pure signs in this picture is so obvious that they have a far greater power of making us see things than ever a naturalistic painting could have. In the dark rhythm of this pictorial communication it is these signs which transmit the artist's message. We have discovered all this solemnly inscribed within a picture of lapidary simplicity.

The message which Klee transcribed at the dictate of that far-off voice was grave, but in order to understand how grave we must take account of his physical condition. For all Klee's spiritual communications corresponded to something which was happening on the physical plane. His images originated in and were nourished by this spiritual-physical unity; from it they derived warmth and humanity as well as the power to evoke new pictures which, although they might be disguised as mythical reflections of the human race, nevertheless reflected the contemporary world. Charon's boat—in ancient times it was a symbol for the journey into darkness and oblivion, the symbol of death. Klee was very ill. His illness had become malignant in 1935 already, and for a long time he had been living in the shadow of death, his own death, which was a slow process like the withering of a plant. There were no crises, no periods of heroic resistance; Klee just faded away like a leaf in autumn when the sap runs dry. Is there not something curious about the fact that Klee suffered from a mysterious illness which no doctor was able to diagnose, so that he died of a slow drying up of his vital juices, of a progressive failure in the functioning of his glands and mucous membranes? The inevitability of this, so to speak, vegetable death produced a certain seriousness in the pictures of his last years. Gone is the good-humoured laughter which had hitherto permeated the whole of his art. His forms too were affected by his seriousness, and if we pass from the dimension of content to that of form we are almost shocked by the extreme economy with which he now handles colour and line.

This seriousness is common to all Klee's late pictures, and it first appeared when he moved to the little studio in Bern, that cell where he performed his final meditations. It is clearly visible in the images which Klee now found within himself, which come from the darker regions of his imago and often have the appearance of magic spells. '*Demonic*' is the title of one of them, while others are called '*Outbreak of Fear*', '*Monster in Readiness*', '*Dame Demon*', '*Early Sorrow*', and '*Death and Fire*'. But there are also '*The Creator*', '*The Penitent*', '*Saint out of a Window*'—and then the series of Angels. As his forms became increasingly larger, so did the size of Klee's pictures, until canvases of between three and six feet long were almost the rule. Even the delicately coloured water-colours in which Klee had previously depicted his microcosm, suddenly became harsh and simplified: a broadly washed-in background with a drawing on top of it in lines as bold as those of hieroglyphics. The microcosm exists no more, for even the drawing, to whose delicate fabric Klee transmitted the most minute stirring of which he was aware, was now reduced to a simple hieroglyphic, a sign suggesting by graphic means a content and a meaning. This type of pictorial writing is as abstract as the descriptive sounds in speech. The large black signs do not depict the object; they appear on the page like a written communication, but they are abstract hieroglyphics which only have meaning by analogy.

Thus Klee's whole technique was transformed. Instead of fine paper he began to use a coarse parchment; and for his oil paintings he gave up using fine canvas and resorted to coarse sacking. He also used newspaper (which had always fascinated him) in some of his large canvases. Klee had always treated water-colour as a rich and liquid medium, so much so in fact that rather than draw on it directly he had resorted to the indirect means of drawing through an ink-covered intermediary sheet. Suddenly however Klee seems to have been troubled by the richness of this medium. He then turned to the coarsest possible medium, poster paints, which he applied as a background and then with a coarse brush drew signs on top of it in black. Thus Klee reduced everything to the simplest formula, abandoned small-scale compositions, and allowed his compressed forms and areas of space to expand into simple broad planes. Asceticism became the monk, and his pictures were dressed in a hairshirt.

Yet despite the asceticism Klee's colours shine out with a mystic glow. Indeed on the formal plane the most sensational development in Klee's work during the last years of his life is the new force which his colours acquired through simplification. And because the mystic dimension is attained through colour, all that has to be read is contained in the monumental black hieroglyphics. Like leads in a stained glass window these magic black signs bring out the maximum of luminosity in the colours and give them a similar mystic significance. These pictures are like the carpets and silk banners hung up in Mohammedan mosques to remind the faithful of the unspeakable power of the words of the Koran. Prayer-rugs on which are inscribed formulas for meditation—Klee's late pictures open the door to a world of experience as infinite as that.

It was in about 1937 that colour in Klee's pictures was freed from all restraint and entrusted alone with the task of creating an element of mysticism. The illumination from within, the growing power of colour to point the way to that eternity 'which used to be symbolized by the halo'. This led straight to things unearthly. But even unearthly objects can only be made

concrete with worldly materials. Illumination from within—
Klee discovered the appropriate means. He resorted to working on linen with pastel, a medium whose soft granules of
colour gave him the effect he wanted—a velvety depth, an
interior glow, a translucency like stained glass.[1] It was not
long before he was also able to produce resonance in depth by
means of a peculiar technique of building up one layer of
colour on another. He would take a piece of coarse sacking
and paint on it a background colour in tempera; at once the
combination of the rough surface and the dry medium produced a certain resonance in depth. Over this he would then
apply a wash of brighter colour—yellow ochre over dark brown
for example—covering only the uppermost surface of the
threads of the canvas. The coarse hair shirt of the canvas made
his colours shine out with a new reality: immaterial, blended
by light, but yet like a jewel which breaks up light rays and
returns them transformed into a new reality.

Then there was the increase of colour. During this final
period Klee preferred colours which are close together on the
chromatic circle, because such colours blend without a
struggle, support each other, and thus contribute their full
radiance to the final colour. Many of Klee's late pastels are
based on passages from one colour to the next, for example
from yellow through orange to terracotta, or from yellow-
green to dark green, and so on. Their composition is for the
most part based on a series of simple cubes which are either
divided from each other, or at any rate rhythmically stamped,
by black lines which frequently have no objective trait. And
mere colour descriptions provide their titles. Thus one picture
is called 'Green on Green', and another 'Signs in Yellow'. Klee

---

[1] It is worth noting that, in his search for a way of giving colour its fullest expressive value, Adolf Hölzel (1853–1934) also resorted to pastel.

found that working with complementaries, or traversing the chromatic circle diagonally, produced a span so great as to create a balance which was too static to dispel the strife between the opposing colours. '*Harmonized Strife*' is the title Klee gave to a pastel in which the span from orange to violet is harmonized and transposed into an overall tonality of light gold.

But sometimes a wide colour-span led to an objective event which necessitated a daring activity among the vividly glowing colours. A picture of this sort is entitled '*Revolt of the Viaduct*'. Things happen against a violet background: one unit of a viaduct has stepped out of formation and has begun to advance. Each unit is a concise sign: a rounded arch with a bit of roadway on top of it. But the two piers of each arch have been given little feet so that they are able to walk. They form up in frontal aspect for their demonstration, the back ranks pushing against the jammed middle ranks, while the front rank is stepping boldly out towards the spectator. A man-made construction has thus renounced its role at the service of humanity and is advancing on us doing a goose-step of its own. The advance of these objects is menacing and it is advisable to make room for them or to run away. Yet escape into the picture is absolutely impossible, for the roadway crossing the viaduct has been completely destroyed and, as a result of the interruption of the arch-borne continuity, the bits of roadway merely lead to a labyrinthine confusion. The violet world of the background appears metaphorically pitiless and without exit. The colour has a threatening glow. The object in revolt is dressed in the most active colours. Its deepest tonality is dark madder; from there it strides on through red to yellow, culminating in the foremost rank in an angry cadmium yellow. The dangerous span from violet to a red moving towards cadmium reveals the hidden menace behind the colour-symbolism. The revolutionary colours are kept in check by black lines, so that the violet of the background does not steal any of their penetrating force. Thus the angry colours have a pure glow which seems to come from within themselves: the colour of revolt. The threat prevails over the joke, the image is a reflection of the period. This picture was painted in 1937, at the same time as Picasso's '*Guernica*', when bombs were raining down on Spain. In that year, those who had not succumbed to the lies of politicians became aware for the first time of their powerlessness to oppose the destructive menace of machines. Fate pressed inexorably on. The established order everywhere was upset, and machines were let loose to wreak their destructive work and reduce the civilized world to a pile of rubble.

Was there still a home on this earth for Klee? The attractions of the world beyond seemed to counsel departure. Yet he went on with his poetic creations, full, ripe and overflowing with manly spiritual melancholy. 1938 was a year which witnessed a golden pictorial harvest in the form of a series of very large, radiant pictures. The '*Fruits in Blue*' gleam golden yellow like jewels set off against a background of lapis-lazuli. '*Pomona Over-ripe*' consists of fat black signs against a reddish-orange autumnal background. Then there is '*The Park at Lu*', with its bright, luminous background—emerald green, light ochre, pale grey, brownish-red, orange and raspberry—on which are inscribed black hieroglyphics signifying fruit-trees, with a graceful exotic conifer in the middle. Here and there a few paths wind gently across the surface, being arranged so as to catch the eye and carry it into the far-off dreamland of this garden. There is even a remote but blessed island—'*Insula Dulcamara*'. In this a spring-like background of pale pink, a slightly warm green and an aerial blue spreads freely across the enormous surface (six feet). It is a vision of the first spring on an island inhabited by gods, and the artist's brush has traced the simple words of the poem in rhythmically drawn black signs on top of this background. The long cool shore of the island; its friendly, small vegetation amidst which is one large other-worldly plant, and wavy lines which wind through the fields—snakes, the sacred animals which inhabit this distant land. Far away in the background a ship steams across the sea, leaving a dark constellation which is sinking behind it as it moves towards a light one which is rising. Oh, far-off land!

But the last traces of worldliness were only waiting to disappear. In 1939 Klee's forms underwent a sudden upheaval; their outlines became rounded and taut to the point of bursting. The objective signs describe a world luxuriant, overflowing and bloated with excess, which crudely airs its slimy, sexual side. Here all worldly ties have been cut, for behind the unwholesome repletion of this *horror vacui* lurks corruption, there is a '*Monster in Readiness*' or '*Demons*'. Yet the decomposition of this unwholesome world is offset by the birth of creatures which refuse to belong to it. A whole hierarchy of angels makes its appearance: '*Archangel*', '*Angelus Militans*', '*Vigilant Angel*', '*Angel Overflowing*', '*Angel from a Star*'. And on one occasion the words in Klee's mind formed themselves into a childish couplet, which haunted him till it had been written down:

> *Einst werd ich liegen im Nirgend*
> *Bei einem Engel Irgend.*[1]

This host of angels stood by Klee's side and were his com-

---

[1] A play on words which is untranslatable into English. An approximation to the sense might be:

> *One of these days I shall lie in nothingness*
> *Beside an angel of some kind.*

panions on the last part of his journey. Klee was always at his ease in intermediate realms and loved to flit from one to another. He regarded coloured forms as the most direct means of effecting his transitions, and by virtue of their magic he was able to pass from things earth-bound to those moving in the cosmos, from things inorganic to things organic, from things growing to things moving, from plants to animals and so on to man. Change was the root of all being, and every sort of possibility was latent in reality. On the religious plane the greatest possibility for worldly metamorphosis lay with the angels, and in his final meditations Klee sought to penetrate that intermediate realm in which they live. He was far too modest, far too conscious of the laws governing his growth on this earth to aspire to the heights on which gods sit. He was no Prometheus, but a devoted slave who perhaps had a glimpse of the All-Holy on his distant throne because he sought to keep close to the heart of all creation. If only he could look down just once more like the 'old grey-beard' on some coastline![1] God was too far away, but his love was manifested in the functioning of his creatures. Why then, Klee asked himself, should he seek to break out of the warm circle of creation, whose boundaries are watched over by angels, and attempt to reach the realm of the All-Highest where no further change was possible? Klee's religious sentiment was closely tied to reality, to the idea of creation as a divine reality made manifest, God himself being unapproachable although apprehensible by analogy within the circle of created things. All worldly things had in them, for Klee, a spark of the divine and were thus infinitely mobile. And on the circumference of the vast circle of creation stood the angels—among them one which would be his, the 'Engel Irgend'.

[1] A reference to a picture of 1938 by Klee entitled *Greybeard and the Coastline*.

DRUMMER, 1940
Klee Foundation

DEATH AND FIRE, 1940
Klee Foundation

TOWARDS THE ANGELS

When colour took on a mystic quality during Klee's final meditations, the door to eternity was opened. And Klee's last pictures are festive images whose colour has a far-off radiance. One is called *'Glass Façade'*, another *'Watchman on High'*, and yet another *'Saint out of a Window'*. They are all mystic images, variations on a final theme, that of a being whose earthly light is going out but who is nevertheless irradiated from a source in some other world.

When Klee died on 29th June 1940 at Muralto near Locarno, all his work was done. His death was in no way violent; quite simply, his light was extinguished for he had reached the frontier. In an obituary tribute Georg Schmidt referred to Klee's last works as 'Variations on the theme "The End—period"', and nothing could be more true. Klee's whole life was governed by his acceptance of things as they are. Death was within him for a long while, and he accepted that too. He knew he was about to die. If we now look back again at the picture called *'Dark Voyage'* we can see the import of its message even more clearly: the Ship of the Dead on the journey to Oblivion. But now we can also guess where the voyage will end. It will not be in the blind alley of the question mark. His unlocated home in nothingness will be where the final line is drawn, beside an angel of some kind.

BIBLIOGRAPHY

Practically every pre-1945 publication in which the work of Klee is mentioned will be found listed in the Bibliography of the Paul Klee Catalogue of the Museum of Modern Art, New York (3rd edition, 1946). Among later publications the most important are two portfolios of colour plates with text by Georg Schmidt published by the Holbein Verlag (Basle, 1946 and 1949); another published by the Verlag Benteli (Bern, 1949); also a new edition of the second volume of Will Grohmann's *The Drawings of Paul Klee*, published by Müller and Kiepenheuer, (Bergen, 1948). In 1948 appeared also a small but sensitive book by Hans Friedrich Geist (Hauswedell, Hamburg), which contains a more up-to-date bibliography. The Swiss review *Werk* contained in its number of June 1950 an important article by the same author: 'Paul Klee and the World of the Child'. In 1949, Douglas Cooper published a small illustrated volume on Klee (Penguin Books, London). Among the many exhibition catalogues of recent years the following have particular documentary value: two catalogues compiled by Ludwig Grote for exhibitions in Munich, *Der Blaue Reiter* (1949) and *Painters at the Bauhaus* (1950); the catalogue of the exhibition *Late Works of Paul Klee* held at the Düsseldorfer Kunstsammlungen in 1948, which contains notes by some of Klee's pupils; the catalogue of *Paintings, drawings and prints by Paul Klee from the Klee Foundation, Bern, with additions from American Collections* published by the Museum of Modern Art, New York (1949); the catalogue of the exhibition to commemorate the tenth anniversary of Klee's death organized by the Kunstmuseum, Basle (1950), which contains a reprint of a funeral oration by Georg Schmidt delivered on 5th July 1940. But the finest and most important document is a contribution by Paul Klee himself, his lecture *On Modern Art* (*Über die moderne Kunst*) delivered at the Museum of Jena in 1924, (German text published by Verlag Benteli, Bern, in 1945; English translation by Faber and Faber, London, 1949).

Other books recently published in English (not available to the author when his book was in preparation).

Pedagogical Sketchbook by Paul Klee; introduction and translation by Sibyl Moholy-Nagy (Faber and Faber, London; Praeger, New York 1953)

Paul Klee by Carola Giedion-Welcker (Faber and Faber, London; The Viking Press, New York 1952)

Paul Klee I by Herbert Read (Faber Gallery Series, London 1948)

Paul Klee II by Andrew Forge (Faber Gallery Series, London 1954)

INDEX

Apollinaire, 57, 87
Aragon, 87
Architecture, 151–2
Arp, 87, 139

Baargeld, 87
Bach, 22
Barlach, 28
Baumeister, 134
Beardsley, Aubrey, 38
Bergson, Henri, 164
Blaue Reiter, 50, 51–5
Boccioni, 59
Bonnard, 41
Braque, Georges, 53, 55, 71, 87, 107, 142
Breton, André, 87, 120, 138, 140, 141, 142
Breton landscape painters, 26

Candide (Voltaire), 48–9, 54, 76
Carrà, Carlo, 59, 61, 90
Carus, Carl Gustav, 150, 160
Caspar, 50
Cézanne, 45, 49, 55, 56, 65, 88, 108, 116, 137, 168, 170
Charenton, Enguerrand, 194
Children, art of, 49–50
Chirico, de, 139
Cockburnspath, Scottish school of, 26
Constructivism, 166–75
Corrinth, C., Potsdamer Platz oder die Nächte des Neuen Messias, 76–7

Cubism, 55–8, 88–9, 135
Dadaism, 87–8
de la Fresnaye, 55
Delacroix, 125
Delaunay, Robert, 22, 55, 57, 58, 61, 69, 73, 108, 172, 179
Derain, 55
Dohrn, zoologist, 30
Dill, Ludwig, 26 n.
Duchamp, Marcel, 87

Eluard, 87
Ende, Hans am, 26 n.
Endell, August, 27
Ensor, James, 40
Ernst, Max, 87, 139
Etymology, 146
Expressionism, 26–7

Fauve movement, 55
Feininger, Lyonel, 78, 81, 183, 191
Fra Angelico, 194
Friedrich, C. D., 150
Futurists, Italian, 59

Gauguin, Paul, 22, 131, 137
Geist, H. F., 114
Giacometti, Giovanni, 116
Gleizes, 58
Goethe, 136, 150–61
Goltz, Hans, 55, 76
Goya, 39
Gris, Juan, 135–8

O

INDEX

Gropius, Walter, 77–8, 80, 165, 183
Grosz, 87
Grünewald, 114

Haller, Hermann, 29, 150–1
Hausenstein, 76
Heidegger, 122
Hesse, Hermann, 125, 134
Hodler, 36
Hölzel, Adolf, 22, 26 n., 28, 78, 200 n.
Imagery, poetic, 130–2
Imago, the, 160–4
Italian Futurists, 59–62
Itten, Johannes, 78

Jugendstil movement, 22, 27–9

Kaesbach, 183, 192
Kafka, Franz, 88, 118, 120
Kandinsky, 22, 28, 51, 52, 54, 55, 58, 61, 78, 81, 82–3, 93, 127, 183, 191
Kant, 136, 154
Klee, Felix (son), 40, 49
Klee, Hans (father), 19, 21
Klee, Paul
   birth and antecedents, 19–21
   musical education and virtuosity, 21–23
   general education, and love of Greek and French classical literature, 23
   first essays in drawing, 23–5
   enters Knirr's school in Munich, 25
   influenced by artistic movement in Munich of 1890's, 25–9
   leaves Knirr's, and studies under Stuck, 29
   visits Italy with Hermann Haller, 29–33, 150–1
   settles in Bern, 33
   attempt to gain technical mastery, 34–6
   and Nature and pure form, 36–8
   and tonal values, and influence of Goya, 38–9
   awareness of confidence, 39–40

Klee, Paul (*continued*)
   marriage, move to Munich, and birth of son, 40
   impact of Van Gogh, 41, 47–8, 49
   and construction and psychic improvisation, 41–4
   influence of Cézanne, 45, 170
   and colour, 44–5, 58, 63–74, 107–8, 171–4, 179, 200–1, 205
   first small successes, and approach by Kubin, 45–7
   and the art of children, 49–50
   joins Sema group, 50
   joins the Blaue Reiter, 51–5
   and Cubism, 56–8
   and the Futurists, 59–62
   visit to Tunis, 63–7
   war service, and demobilization, 70–1
   and synthesis of the constructive and dynamic, 71–4
   established fame, 76–7
   teacher at Bauhaus, 77–83, 183, 184
   teacher at Düsseldorf Academy of Fine Arts, 80–1, 183–4
   system of teaching, 83–6, 113–14
   and Dadaism, 87–8
   and the questioning of objects 89–91
   his *Pedagogical Sketchbook*, and mastery of formal means, 92–109
   and the study of Nature, 110–24
   and the transmutation of visual images into higher symbols, 125–30
   and poetic imagery, 130–2
   and formative origin and process of creation, 132–45
   and Surrealism, 139–44
   visit to Egypt, 148, 149, 162–3
   and Goethe's romanticism, 150–60
   and the imago, 160–4
   and memory, 163–4
   striving for the spiritual, 165–6
   and constructivism, 166–75
   and perspectival pictures, 167–8
   and original repetitions of motif and rhythm, 175–8

INDEX

Klee, Paul (*continued*)
  and use of parallel bands, 178–9
  and air and space, 179–87
  and *pointillisme*, 187–9
  his achievement, 190
  dismissal from Düsseldorf Academy,
    and return to Bern, 191–2
  and a new world culture, 192–4
  and the world beyond, 194–205
  illness, 197–8
  transformation of technique near end
    of his life, 198–202
  his death, 205
  Paintings, Drawings etc.
  Adrasta Polis, 176
  Aged Phoenix, 38
  Alarming Moment, An (reproduc-
    tion), 44
  Allegory of the Mountain, 38
  Autumnal Place, 81–2, 166
  Balcony, The, 41
  Before the Snow, 181
  Being Young, 176
  Beetle (reproduction), 31
  Bern (reproduction), 20
  Big Dome, The (reproduction), 156
  Candide illustrations (reproductions),
    13, 48–9, 54, 76
  Cat Acrobats (reproduction), 169
  City of the Lagoons (reproduction),
    184–5
  Classical Gardens, 176
  Classical Seaboard, 188
  Cock and the Grenadier, The, 167
  Comedian, 36
  Composition with a Window, 71
  Concert on a Branch (reproduction),
    24
  Corrinth's *Potsdamer Platz* illustra-
    tions, 76–7, (reproduction) 79
  Creator, The, 166
  Dame Demon, 166
  Dark Voyage, 196–7, 205
  Exercitium in Blue and Orange, 175
  Female Grace, 38

Fire Wind, 170
Fish in the Brook, 116, (reproduc-
  tion), 117
Fishes, 110–12, 115, 124, 155
Flying Seed (reproduction), 152–3
Fool in a Trance, 177
Fruits in Blue, 200
Full Moon, The, 71–3, 82, 167
Klee, Paul (*continued*)
  Garden of Passion, 62
  Glass Façade, 205
  Glimpse of the Land of Plenty, 147,
    148–9
  Going to the Dance of the Fly-By-
    Nights (reproduction), 75
  Grey beard and the Coastline, 204 *n.*
  Growth of Nocturnal Plants, 170
  Harmonized Strife, 201
  Hat, Lady and Little Table, 166
  Hero with a Wing, 38, 48
  Heroic Bowing, 23
  High way and Byways, 147–8, 178
  Higher, then dwindling (*Potsdamer
    Platz* series, reproduction), 79
  Hovering, 182, 185–6
  In the Temple of Flora, 176
  Inclined Blooms (reproduction),
    136–7
  Inside the Body's Cavern (reproduc-
    tion), 195
  Insula Dulcamara, 202–3
  Kairuan (reproduction), 67
  Landscape UOL, 188
  Light and Other Things, 188
  Menacing Head, 38
  Mildly Tropical Landscape, 63–4,
    68–70
  Mixed Weather, 181
  Monarchist, 38
  Moonrise, 127–8, 175–6
  Mosaic of the City Proun, 189
  Mount of the Bull, The, 172
  Necropolis, 147
  New Perseus, 38
  North Room, 186–8, 189

INDEX

Klee, Paul (*continued*)
  Oceanic Landscape, 181
  Open-air Still-life, 188
  Over and Up (reproduction), 193
  Park at Lu, The, 202
  Pause-Sign, Drawing with the (reproduction), 91
  Plants, for Earth and Air (reproduction), 123
  Playful Water, 114
  Pomona Over-ripe, 202
  Ptarmigans, 170
  Rayleaf Plants, 176
  Revolt of the Viaduct, 201–2
  Rising and Gliding, 182
  Rooster and the Grenadier, The, 71
  Saint out of a Window, 205
  Scene from an Aerial Hunt, 181
  Schriftbilder, 70
  Silver-Moon Chimes, 170
  Spirits of the Air, 180
  Stag (reproduction), 80
  Storm, 181
  Suicide on a Bridge, 62
  Town Sailing, A, 182
  Virgin in a Tree, 36
  Watchman on High, 205
  Ways of Studying Nature, schematic drawing in (reproduction), 121
  Woman and Animal, 35–6, second version, 38
Klee-Frick, Ida Maria (mother), 19, 20
Kleist, 37
Knirr's art school, Munich, 25
Kubin, 45–7
Künstlervereinigung group, 55

Langhammer, Arthur, 26 *n.*
Langhammer, Karl, 26 *n.*
Le Fauconnier, 55
Léger, 134
Leonardo da Vinci, 134

Macke, August, 52, 53, 54, 61, 64, 65, 172

Mackensen, Fritz, 26 *n.*
Mallarmé, 138
Marc, Franz, 52, 53, 54, 59, 61–2, 118–19, 131, 149
Marcks, Gerhardt, 78
Masson, 134, 139
Mataré, 134
Matisse, 22, 53, 55, 61, 116
Mehring, 87
Memory, 163–4
Merck, 136
Meyer, Adolf, 78
Meyer, Hannes, 80, 183
Michael Angelo, 31
Miró, 134, 139
Modersohn, Otto, 26 *n.*
Modersohn, Paula, 27
Moholy-Nagy, 78
Moilliet, Louis, 39, 51, 64, 65
Mondrian, Piet, 77, 168, 171
Morgenstern, 131
Mozart, 22
Muche, Georg, 78
Müller, Georg, 76
Munich, artistic movement of 1890's in, 25–9

Nerval, Gérard de, 125
Nolde, Emil, 27, 117
Novalis, 119

Objects
  questioning of, 88–91
  natural, 120–2
  and combination of forms, 132–9
  humanization of, 150–60
Oppenheimer, 50
Orphic Cubism, 58
Overbeck, Fritz, 26 *n.*

Pascin, 40
Paul, Jean, 74
Perspectival pictures, 167–8
Perpective, 90
Picabia, 87

INDEX

Picasso, 53, 55, 87, 107, 116, 134, 139, 142
Piero di Cosimo, 134
Pittura Metafisica, Italian, 89
Poetic imagery, 130–2
Pointillisme, 187–9
Proust, Marcel, 89, 121, 164

Ray, Man, 87, 139
Reverdy, Pierre, 141
Ribemont-Dessaignes, 87
Rilke, Rainer Maria, 88, 121–2, 143, 162
Rimbaud, 138
Romanticism, 125, 126, 150–60
Rouault, 55
Rousseau, Henri, 55
Runge, 125, 150
Russolo, 59

Saxe-Weimar, Grand Duke of, 77–8
Scharff, 50
Schinkel, 152
Schlegel, 125, 150
Schlemmer, Oskar, 78, 81, 183, 191
Schlichter, 87
Schmidt, Georg, 192, 205
Schreyer, Lothar, 78
Schmuz-Baudiss, 28
Schwitters, Kurt, 87

Sema (The Sign) Group, 50
Seurat, 187
Severini, 59
Stuck, 29
Stumpf, Lili (wife), 40
Sung-Ti, 134
Surrealism, 139–44

Tzara, Tristan, 87

Valéry, Paul, 120
Valloton, 41
van de Velde, 27, 77
Van Gogh, 22, 41, 47–8, 49, 65, 174
Vienna Sezession (Klimt), 36
Vlaminck, 55
Vuillard, 41

Walden, Herwarth, 54, 59
Warburg, Aby, 164
Ways of Studying Nature, Klee's essay on, 120–1
Wedderkop, 76
Wilde, Oscar, 39
Witz, Konrad, 194
Wolff, Kurt, 76
Worpswede school, 26–7

Zahn, Leopold, 76